BRAIN GAMES®

50 States
100 Puzzles

pil

Publications International, Ltd.

Let's get social!

 @Publications_International

@PublicationsInternational

@BrainGames.TM

www.pilbooks.com

Puzzles from the U.S.A.

Discover fun facts about the fifty states! *Brain Games*®
50 States 100 Puzzles includes two puzzles for each
state. You'll find an assortment of word puzzles like
anagrams, crosswords, and word searches, logic puzzles
that will have you figuring out travel itineraries within
a state, visual puzzles like dot-to-dots featuring a state
icon, trivia puzzles about state symbols, landmarks, and
famous residents, and memory puzzles about festivals
and history. As you solve, you'll refresh your knowledge
about famous Americans, sports teams, landmarks, and
more! This puzzle collection is the perfect way to take a
virtual trip around the country and celebrate its cities,
natural wonders, small towns, and history. If you need a
hint, an answer key is found at the back of the book!

Awesome Alabama

Across

1. Gossip mag. subject
5. Produce very quickly
11. Cannon or stock follower
12. Barracks no-show
14. John Legend "All ____"
15. Lay claim forcibly
17. Go by yacht
18. Old indoor light source
20. Hitchhiker's request
23. County fair sounds
26. Awkward brute
27. Geologists' studies
29. Shoe section
31. Allow
33. Descended from the same mother
34. High-priced ticket option
35. Like a bubble bath
37. Doubter's reply
38. Early anti-communist
42. Sunk fence
44. Aggressive advertising
47. "How ____ Your Mother"
48. Highland Gaelic
49. Omega symbolizes it
50. Lab tube
51. Soak

Down

1. Down's flower insignia
2. Academic conclusion
3. "____ Miserables"
4. Exotic vacation spot
5. Perturb
6. Larger forearm bone
7. The state is known for it
8. "Children ____ Lesser God" (1986)
9. Alaskan vessel
10. Contact no.
13. Firmly formed
16. Montgomery is its capital
19. Mournful murmur
21. Lithium-____ battery
22. Stuck together
24. Prominent one
25. "____ Alabama"
28. Springs back, as a gun
30. Deposits, as eggs
32. Bigger than med.
36. Savory flavor of glutamates
39. Aid the shady
40. Coin classification
41. Klondike vehicle
42. Groovy
43. Sophisticated
45. The Astros, on scoreboards
46. Sighs of delight

Answers on page 144.

Roll Tide

Change just one letter on each line to go from the top word to the bottom word. Do not change the order of the letters. You must have a common English word at each step.

ROLL

_____

_____

_____

TIDE

Bonus:
Can you find another option?

ROLL

_____

_____

_____

TIDE

About the Iditarod

How much do you know about the Iditarod Trail Sled Dog Race?

1. In what month does the race usually take place?
   - A. January
   - B. February
   - C. March
   - D. It depends on snowfall.

2. The race starts in _____ and ends in _____.
   - A. Anchorage, Nome
   - B. Juneau, Nome
   - C. Nome, Anchorage
   - D. Juneau, Anchorage

3. The course record holder finished the race in 20 days, 0 hours.
   - _____ True
   - _____ False

4. The sled dog that is voted the best dog of the race is given this award.
   - A. Golden Sled
   - B. Golden Harness
   - C. Balto Memorial
   - D. Red Lantern

Answers on page 144.

Searching Alaska

How much do you know about the Iditarod Trail Sled Dog Race? Every word listed is contained within the group of letters. Words can be found in a straight line horizontally, vertically, or diagonally. They may be read either forward or backward.

ALASKA

ANCHORAGE

ARCTIC

BEAUFORT SEA

BERING STRAIT

BOWHEAD WHALE

CHUKCHI SEA

DENALI

DOG MUSHING

ENERGY

EXCLAVE

FAIRBANKS

FISHING

FRONTIER

GLACIERS

GRIZZLY BEAR

IDITAROD

JUNEAU

KENAI
(peninsula)

KING SALMON

MOOSE

NATIVES

NON-CONTIGUOUS

PACIFIC

WILDLIFE

WRANGELL
(mountains)

```
T C R A D O R A T I D I J V C
K E N A I G L A C I E R S Y I
G S D O G M U S H I N G B R T
N T U S A R M O O S E N E E C
A A I O K E I Y K A N I L G R
W L T A U N S Z N L E H A A A
P I A I R G A I Z A R S H R L
A A L S V T I B H L G I W O L
C N A D K E S T R C Y F D H E
I N O M L A S G N I K B A C G
F R O N T I E R N O A U E N N
I L A N E D F X J I C F H A A
C J U N E A U E G U R N W C R
J G W E X C L A V E N E O M W
P P A E S T R O F U A E B N L
```

Answers on page 144.

Cryptograms are messages in substitution code. Break the code to read the message. For example, THE SMART CAT might become FVO QWGDF JGF if **F** is substituted for **T, V** for **H, O** for **E**, and so on.

BUL LPXK HJUSL QFEWUJ FN ESLMJU JUCSXE SK

XL EFQ XK. WF EFLPXEH LF CSJ XLK HJSEWUMJ,

KMDBXCXLV SEW BFOUBXEUKK. VFM ZSEEFL XCGJFOU

FE XL. DML QPSL VFM ZSE WF XK LF AUUG XL NFJ

VFMJ ZPXBWJUE, VFMJ ZPXBWJUE'K ZPXBWJUE,

SEW SBB QPF ZFCU SNLUJ VFM, SK LPU FEU HJUSL

KXHPL QPXZP UOUJV SCUJXZSE KPFMBW KUU.

—LPUFWFJU JFFKUOUBL

Read the story, then turn the page.

Arizona would be short one giant hole in the ground if it weren't for a 160-foot meteorite landing in the northern desert about 50,000 years ago, which left an impact crater about 3,900 feet wide and 560 feet deep. Known today as the Meteor Crater, the site is now a popular tourist attraction. Scientists believe the meteorite that caused the crater was traveling about 28,600 miles per hour when it struck Earth, causing an explosion about 150 times more powerful than the Hiroshima atomic bomb. The meteorite itself probably melted in the explosion, spreading a mist of molten nickel and iron across the surrounding landscape. Fragments of the meteorite are called Canyon Diablo meteorites; the Holsinger meteorite is the largest, with a diameter of more than two feet.

The site has also been called the Barringer Crater, after the family that owns the Barringer Crater Company that owns the land. In the early 1900s, an engineer named Daniel Barringer suggested that the crater was caused by a meteor impact; his company purchased the land around the site.

The site became a National Natural Landmark in 1967. Astronauts trained there in the 1960s and 1970s.

(Do not read this until you have read the previous page!)

1. The crater is wider than it is deep.

_____ True

_____ False

2. The meteor landed about this long ago.

   A. 10,000 years

   B. 20,000 years

   C. 50,000 years

   D. 80,000 years

3. The largest meteorite fragment found from the site is known by this name.

   A. Canyon Diablo

   B. Holsinger

   C. Barringer

   D. Arizona

4. The site is a:

   A. National Park

   B. National Monument

   C. National Natural Landmark

   D. None of the above

Arkansas Anagrams

Unscramble each word or phrase below to reveal a word, phrase, or name related to Arkansas.

CIAO AT UH
(Mountain range)

BE LINEN VOLT
(City serving as Walmart headquarters)

BLOC LINT INN
(Famous politician)

BONBON TRILBY LOTH
(Famous actor born in AR)

OH JAN SYNCH
(Famous singer born in AR)

CRIB KINGDOM
(State bird)

HOG SPRINGS
(National Park)

ADDS RILL
(Department store chain headquartered in Little Rock)

Answers on page 144.

All About Arkansas

BLANCHARD SPRINGS
(Caverns)

BUFFALO RIVER

CRATER OF DIAMONDS
(State Park)

CROWLEY'S RIDGE
(State Park)

FORT SMITH

HERMAN DAVIS
(State Park)

HOBBS
(State Park)

JONESBORO

LITTLE ROCK

MAMMOTH SPRING

OUACHITA

OZARKS

PEA RIDGE

PETIT JEAN
(State Park)

PINE BLUFF

REGNAT POPULUS
(The People Rule)

SOYBEANS

THE NATURAL STATE

TIMBERLANDS

WALMART

N A E J T I T E P E U N Z T E B
M A M M O T H S P R I N G R L M
C T H E N A T U R A L S T A T E
H E R M A N D A V I S F N M S Z
U O Z A R K S W F Q K C W L D C
U P E A R I D G E G H W G A N A
O R O B S E N O J A U N R W A A
E B U F F A L O R I V E R W L O
S D N O M A I D F O R E T A R C
F S R Q U L S N A E B Y O S E S
G S U L U P O P T A N G E R B B
I S G O R H T I M S T R O F M B
R W J I X F F U L B E N I P I O
V X N K C O R E L T T I L B T H
Z G O C R O W L E Y S R I D G E
S K F K A N A T I H C A U O K L

Answers on page 145.

Steinbeck Classics

Across

1. Farewell in old Rome
5. Colorado ski resort
10. Letter-shaped structural beam
11. Mail carrier's rounds
12. Steinbeck novel set in Monterey
14. Prepare to propose
15. Got down to Earth
16. Agcy. for entrepreneurs
18. "Eldorado" rock band
19. Steinbeck novel set in the Salinas Valley
23. Pub draft
24. One of the first TV superstations
25. Violas, cellos, etc.: abbr.
27. Clara Barton, notably
31. Steinbeck novel set on a ranch in northern California
33. Left, on a Spanish map
34. Affectedly precious, to Brits
35. Birth-related
36. Dates steadily

Down

1. Falcons quarterback Michael
2. Impose ___ on (outlaw)
3. Bowling alley section
4. Author Hemingway
5. Airport info next to "Dep."
6. Bean used to make miso
7. Inverted a stitch
8. Star, in France
9. Scientific Sir Isaac
13. Funny bone's joint
17. Bid ___ farewell
19. Sheena who sang "U Got the Look" with Prince
20. Gibson of tennis fame
21. Most parched
22. Blows, as a volcano
26. Madrid maiden: abbr.
28. Investment firm T. ___ Price
29. Blade in "The Mikado"
30. Peer group?
32. Conger, for one

The crossword grid with numbered cells:

1	2	3	4	■	5	6	7	8	9
10				■	11				
12				13					
14					■	15			
■	■	■	16		17	■	18		
19	20	21				22			
23			■	24			■	■	■
25			26	■	27		28	29	30
31				32					
33					■	34			
35					■	36			

80
•77
•79
78• •76
81• 45 46• •49 50
130• 47 53
41 48 •51
•127 40• •54
21• •20 •52 •57
17• •55 •58
16 •56
43• •42 13• 12• •59 •61
126 129• 38 82 39 9• •60 •62
•123 128 •83 8• 63 •65
•122 125• •104 37 •36 4• •67 •66 69
•119 •107 •44 5• •64 1• •68 •70 75
124 34• 35 73• 74
•118 121• •108
•131 •111 •31 •30
120•
117• •112
•115
116

33• •32
28• 29
25 •
24•

2. 71. 72
27 •26 23 22 19 18 15. 14. 11. •10 7• •6 3. •175 177
114 113 110 109 106 105 •150 152 154• 156 •157 159 161 163 165 167 169 171 173 176
98• 99• •102 84 •85 151 153 158 160 162 164 166 168 170 172 174 178
100• 103 96 184• •195 155 179
97 95 •94 186 194 •196
•89 90• 91• 187• •185
189• •188
191•

•92 •190 141
183• 192 193 •142 143 140•
198 197 •180 138 139•
199• •200 144 •145 137
88 93• 182• 201• •181 •147 •146
86 149 •148
87
135 136•
134•

•132 133•

Mountain Peak Match

Match the name of each peak found in Colorado to its description.

1. **Mount Elbert**

2. **Blanca Peak**

3. **Mount Harvard**

4. **Pikes Peak**

A. Found in the "Collegiate Peaks" subset of the Sawatch Range

B. Found in the Sangre de Cristo Mountains

C. Named after an explorer whose first name was Zebulon

D. The highest summit in both Colorado and the Rocky Mountains at 14,400 feet

Answers on page 145.

Denver Delight

AVALANCHE
(Ice hockey)

BRONCOS
(Football)

BROWN PALACE HOTEL

BUCKHORN EXCHANGE
(Oldest restaurant)

COORS FIELD

DENVER MINT

ELITCH THEATRE

FRONT RANGE
(Urban Corridor)

JAMES DENVER
(Territorial Governor)

LODO
(Lower Downtown)

MILE HIGH CITY

MILLENNIUM BRIDGE

MOLLY BROWN HOUSE

NUGGETS
(Basketball)

QUEEN CITY
(Of the Plains)

RAPIDS
(Soccer)

RED ROCKS
(Amphitheatre)

ROCKIES
(Baseball)

SOUTH PLATTE
(River Valley)

TATTERED COVER
(Bookstore)

WALL STREET OF THE WEST

```
E S N W X L E X E V N O R L J S N U T
F G K T G L L T Z H L X T E S D U A S
F K D C A J P Q T M C E O B M I G D E
Q P E I O T H V U A E N M N Q P G B W
Y C T R R R T A X E L A A W D A E U E
T J Q T T B D E K Z E P C L D R T C H
I A D N C A M E R A V N H Z A A S K T
C M T I L W E U R E E V C T A V R H F
H E B M A W C H I P D E L I U A A O O
G S Y R F L R O T N I C I O T O K R T
I D V E C U P V O H N P O V D Y S N E
H E V V V P A K L R C E X V G O R E E
E N U N I B C W L G S T L I E Y O X R
L V C E S O C N O R B F I L V R C C T
I E C D X Z L L Z O M M I L I C K H S
M R U O S V Q M H W K J Q E E M I A L
F R O N T R A N G E H B J I L P E N L
M O L L Y B R O W N H O U S E D S G A
H B R O W N P A L A C E H O T E L E W
```

Connecticut Facts

Across

1. Revolutionary War hero from Connecticut who lost his life while spying on the British
10. Chat room chuckle: abbr.
11. Recipe phrase
12. Apartment relative
13. Slowly permeating
15. One of the Disney dwarfs
16. Stock market pessimist
17. Baked clay
19. "Peer Gynt Suite" composer
21. "Like _____ out of hell"
24. Robert E. Lee's org.
25. Eight-armed creatures
27. Notable timespan
29. Connecticut is one
31. Ignited
32. A recurring beat
34. Condition of TV's Monk: abbr.
36. Pinkish wine
37. Gorilla-like
40. Not serious
42. Broadway beginning
45. Second afterthought: abbr.
46. Japanese site of the 1972 Winter Olympics
48. Fully horizontal
49. "How was _____ know?"
50. Calligrapher's item
51. The trunk of this legendary Connecticut tree once served as a hiding place for an important document

Down

1. Winning margin, at times
2. Mater or Gluck
3. Chef's toque, e.g.
4. Suspect's defense
5. Pearly coating
6. Versatile, powerwise
7. Watch
8. Abbr. on a business letter
9. The Fundamental Orders of Connecticut is considered to be the first written document of this kind
10. Popular shellfish sandwich on the East Coast
14. Grps. and assns.
18. Gershwin's "_____ Rhythm"
20. Reaction to poison ivy
22. Daring and fearless
23. Bee-related prefix
24. Coral isles
26. Corp. bosses
28. P on a fraternity house
30. Govt. investigator
33. Fermented soya beans
35. English dude
38. Assume without proof
39. In a huff
41. Madonna's "La _____ Bonita"
43. Club in a Manilow hit
44. Not just a hike
45. Plastic pipe: abbr.
47. "_____ favor, senor!'"

Answers on page 146.

Connecticut Calling

Cryptograms are messages in substitution code. Break the code to read the message. For example, THE SMART CAT might become FVO QWGDF JGF if **F** is substituted for **T, V** for **H, O** for **E,** and so on.

KEAM EQ ZEDDMZLCZOL'K DCZGDSAMK SJM: LRM

ZEDKLCLOLCED KLSLM, LRM DOLAMU KLSLM, LRM

FJEPCKCEDK KLSLM, SDY LRM NSDY EQ KLMSYW

RSICLK.

Delaware Anagrams

Unscramble each word or phrase below to reveal a word, phrase, or name related to Delaware.

ROVED
(Place name)

LOW MINTING
(Place name)

ESTATES THRIFT
(Nickname given to Delaware because of its role in ratifying the U.S. Constitution.)

BE JOINED
(Famous resident)

ENCAMP NINJA NOUN
(Female astronomer from Delaware)

BUN HEEL
(State bird)

REHAB HOE BOTCH
(Vacation destination)

GLIB CYNIC
(State sport)

Answers on page 146.

State Symbols

How much do you know about Delaware?

1. Delaware's state wildlife animal is the:
   A. Grey fox
   B. Skunk
   C. Black bear
   D. Elk

2. Delaware's state tree is the:
   A. Oak
   B. Sugar Maple
   C. American holly
   D. Aspen

3. Delaware's state beverage is:
   A. Beer
   B. Apple cider
   C. Milk
   D. Cranberry juice

4. Delaware's state flower is the:
   A. Azalea
   B. Saguaro cactus blossom
   C. Mountain laurel
   D. Peach blossom

Travel Itinerary

The traveler is visiting five locations in Florida. In alphabetical order, they are: Jacksonville, Miami, Orlando, Tallahassee, and Tampa. Each location will be visited only once. Can you put together the travel timeline, using the information below?

1. Jacksonville is neither the first nor final city visited.

2. The traveler visits the city on the Gulf Coast immediately before going to the city that hosts the Magic (NBA).

3. Florida's state capital is visited sometime before Tampa.

4. The traveler goes from the city that hosts the Marlins (MLB) and the Dolphins (NFL) to another city before proceeding to the city closest to Disney World.

5. The southernmost city that is closest to the Everglades is visited third.

Answers on page 146.

Our Largest Tropical Wilderness

Across

1. Lizard common in the Everglades
6. Everglades reptiles, for short
12. Columbus's birthplace
13. Indians or oranges
14. Highly proficient
15. Prevents, legally
16. Iran's former name
18. Nickname of the Everglades
24. "A wink is as good as ____"
25. Actor Chaney, Jr.
26. Bear false witness
27. Vietnam's ____ Dinh Diem
28. "____ Rosenkavalier": Strauss opera
29. Rating for "South Park"
30. National Scenic Byway that runs through the Everglades
33. Full of foam
34. Fried lightly
37. "Old MacDonald" refrain
41. Words finger-drawn on a dirty car
42. 1983 Indy winner Tom
43. Aquatic salamander common in Florida
44. Bird of the Everglades

Down

1. Spiritual leader ____ Khan IV
2. "The Simpsons" neighbor Flanders
3. Wallet bill
4. Cut off, as branches
5. One feeding
6. Makes an effort
7. Designate, as a seat
8. Genghis Khan was one
9. U.S. scientific satellite of the 60's
10. Dem.'s opposite
11. Hissing sound
17. Person who sets a good example
18. Deliver a diatribe
19. "Young Frankenstein" heroine
20. Va-va-____ (exciting quality)
21. Edison's middle name
22. California's ____ Valley: Reagan Library site
23. Close tightly, as an envelope
28. Risk-taker's challenge
29. Hard on one's patience
31. "____ shoe fits..."
32. Not those
34. Bachelor in personal ads, briefly
35. Non-pro sports org.
36. American currency, as often listed
38. At any time, to a poet
39. "____ Got You Under My Skin"
40. Granola grain

Answers on page 146.

Going to Georgia

ATHENS

ATLANTA

AUGUSTA

BLUE RIDGE MOUNTAINS

BRASSTOWN BALD

BROWN THRASHER
(State bird)

CHEROKEE ROSE
(State flower)

COCA-COLA

COLUMBUS

DELTA

GOLDEN ISLES

JIMMY CARTER

LARGEMOUTH BASS
(State fish)

MACON

MARTIN LUTHER KING, JR.

PEACH STATE

PECANS

PIEDMONT

QUARTZ
(State gemstone)

SAVANNAH

SHARK TOOTH
(State fossil)

SUN BELT

```
R P F Q L W P G N A T N A L T A K B
P J L F I A A E A N Q Y D P J H L A
I Z G S D U R P A I O J J B C U E T
T C R N G L I G U C S C R B E I A L
J Y O U I E A Z E E H O A R C S T E
J J S C D K T B L M W S I M H X H D
Y T I M A R R S N N O D T A Q H E C
A I O M A C I E T W G U R A W B N L
M N Q U M N O H H E O K T C T T S H
T Y Q J E Y R L M T T T F H L E A F
R Q H D K A C O A O U F S E B N H O
U O L T S W U A O O V L B S N A Z T
Q O U H H N P T R R X N N A A Z S R
G V E H T E H Y U T U E V I C R D S
Z R P A C H Y H D S E A B T T Y B G
V Y I A A K U S I J S R E X L R F B
S N N M C H E R O K E E R O S E A I
S S C W W C O L U M B U S L H X S M
```

Peaches and Grits

Change just one letter on each line to go from the top word to the bottom word. Do not change the order of the letters. You must have a common English word at each step.

Did you know? Peaches are Georgia's official state fruit, while grits are the official prepared food. Other state symbols include the peanut (crop) and vidalia sweet onion (vegetable).

P E A C H

_____

_____

_____

_____ These may go awry

_____

_____

_____

_____

_____ To stumble or cause to stumble

_____

G R I T S

Island Hopping

The traveler is visiting five of Hawaii's islands. In alphabetical order, they are: Hawai'i (the Big Island), Kaua'i, Maui, Moloka'i, and Oahu. Each location will be visited only once. Can you put together the travel timeline, using the information below?

1. Moloka'i is visited immediately before the island that is host to Haleakala National Park.

2. The traveler begins on the island that is home to the volanoes Mauna Kea and Mauna Loa.

3. The most populated island is visited sometime after the Big Island, but not immediately after.

4. The home of Waimea Canyon is visited immediately before the island where Honolulu is located.

5. The island where Waikiki Beach is located is not visited last.

Answers on page 147.

Off to Hawaii

Across

1. Short passage
7. College VIP: abbr.
10. "One _____ at a time"
11. Tropical state
12. "It's like _____ here!"
14. Chess or Monopoly
16. Poker hand fee
17. Apple Store buy
18. Pull out
20. Under the weather
21. Protein found in muscles
23. "Are you for _____?"
25. Slanted
27. The Cisco Kid's horse
30. Arrow-shooting Greek god
32. Work, as clay
33. Edison's middle name
35. Nonchalant syllables
37. Airshow trick
38. Said "no contest", e.g.
39. Mayfield's "Move _____"
40. The only city in the US with a royal palace
44. Assertions
45. Honoree spot
46. Nagging pain
47. Annoyed

Down

1. Airport approx.
2. Boomer's baby
3. Numbers cruncher, briefly
4. Thick-skinned grazer
5. Church leader
6. Posted a chirping message
7. The _____, known for its Volcanoes National Park
8. Home of the Marlins
9. One way to pay
10. Helix shape
13. Large dragonfly
15. Part of the retina
18. Broadway legend Hagen
19. Large industry built on 11-Across in the early 1900s
22. Sri Lanka, formerly
24. Self-defense art
26. Frequent Kona and Kohala coastline sight
28. "Luck _____ Lady": "Guys and Dolls" song
29. Extremely unpleasant
31. Dancer with seven veils
33. Simple greeting with a much deeper meaning
34. Guarantee (with "for")
36. Like a thicket
41. "Bad" cholesterol, briefly
42. Oil-rich land: abbr.
43. Yogurt topper

Answers on page 147.

An Idaho Animal

Cryptograms are messages in substitution code. Break the code to read the message. For example, THE SMART CAT might become FVO QWGDF JGF if **F** is substituted for **T, V** for **H, O** for **E,** and so on.

XZDIE'L LMDMP UELLXA XL MIP IDWPKBDC IEKLP, D

OPKV PDKAV PJNXCP MIDM QDL UXKLM ZXLTEOPKPZ

XC IDWPKBDC, XZDIE, FV D TDMMAP KDCTIPK.

MIP UXKLM IDWPKBDC IEKLPL AXOPZ DFENM

3.5 BXAAXEC VPDKL DWE.

Read the story, then turn the page.

The state of Idaho was admitted to the Union in 1890 as the 43rd state. It had been part of the United States since 1846, as part of the Oregon Territory, Washington Territory, and Idaho Territory. The first capital of Idaho Territory was Lewiston, a gold rush town founded in 1861. Several years later, the capital was moved south to Boise in a contentious vote.

The origins of both the name of the state and the name of its capital city, Boise, are somewhat hazy. Boise might derive from the French "Les bois," meaning "the woods."

Were you to call from Lewiston to Boise today, you might want to check your clock first—Idaho is split between two time zones, with Boise in Mountain Time and Lewiston in the Pacific Time Zone.

Idaho has a long history of mining that still goes on today. Silver Valley, in the Coeur d'Alene Mountains, began to be mined in the 1860s, 1870s, and 1880s. Silver, zinc, and lead were all mined from the site, with huge amounts of silver coming from the district in the 1970s. A few mines, including the Lucky Friday Mine, are still active today.

(Do not read this until you have read the previous page!)

1. Idaho became a state in this year.
   - A. 1846
   - B. 1861
   - C. 1880
   - D. 1890

2. Lewiston was the first capital of the state.
   - _____ True
   - _____ False

3. Which statement is true?
   - A. Lewiston is on Mountain time, and Boise on Pacific Time.
   - B. Lewiston is on Pacific Time, and Boise on Mountain Time.
   - C. Both cities are in the Mountain Time Zone.
   - D. Both cities are in the Pacific Time Zone.

4. Silver Valley is found in these mountains.
   - A. Lewiston
   - B. Silver Valley
   - C. Coeur d'Alene
   - D. Lucky Friday

This is a connect-the-dots puzzle page. The dots and their numbers are:

126 123

128
127
129 124 122
130 125   121
117 118

116
115 119 120
114 91
113 112 90 89
111
110 109
132
133 131
108
134 107 106
105
104 103 88 87
101 102
100
96 97

67 64

66 65
69 68 63 62

55
86 85
83 71 60 56 54
84 70 61 57 53 49 52
50
161 160 48 51
163 159 158 94 98 45 44
162 155 157 139 95 93
154 151 156 138 140 135 136
150 144 145 137

73 74
16 92 72 75
17 76 33 34
78 77
9 10

82 81
153 152 59 58
148 149
80 79 47 46 43
164 165 20 22 21 41 42
170 167 18 19 23
171 166 147 146 25 24 35
37 40 39
27 36 31 38
169 168 32 225
172 5 6 15 13 14 26 28 29 30
174 173 182 183 223 224
7 8 181 222 221
4 3 177 179 186 184 220
1 2 11 180 188 185 202
175 178 192 190 189 187 200 201
176 205 193 196 191 197 199
208 194 195 198
210 209 207 206 204 213 212 203 219
211 217 216 214
218 215

39

Answer on page 148.

John Deere

AGRICULTURE

BLACKSMITH

BRANCH HOUSE

CHARLES DEERE

FARMING

GLOBAL

HARROW

HARVESTER

HORSEPOWER

JOSEPH DAIN

ILLINOIS

MODEL D

MOLDBOARD

MOLINE

STEEL PLOW

SULKY PLOW

TRACTOR

TWO-CYLINDER

WAGON

```
B R A N C H H O U S E Z H C K V
T B V G L O B A L N Q A X L X G
E O L X U B S I P T N R N C B P
G R F A H A R V E S T E R K L O
D B E R C E R U T L U C I R G A
J R T E E K W W O R R A H I T G
O P A W D C S U E P A Z D W X S
S R M O B S W M I K C D O A W U
E E B P B U E L I M M C C O R L
P F J E U D L L O T Y X L N R K
H S A S V I L D R L H P L O E Y
D X Z R N V E O I A L A T G N P
A J I O M L S N M E H C Q A I L
I D I H D I D F E A A C S W L O
N S O O J E N T P R P D M K O W
C C D O R J S G T Q L C S B M M
```

Indianapolis 500

Unscramble each word or phrase below to reveal a word, phrase, or name related to the famous automobile race.

YES PAWED
(Location)

BAD CRY IRK
(Nickname)

HURRAY ROAN
(First winner in 1911)

SEEKER PRONG
(Owns the Indianapolis Motor Speedway)

BITE FOLK MOLT
(Victory lane tradition)

BARN GROWER
(Name of trophy)

MAYORAL DIME
(Traditional weekend the race is held)

REKINDLE PRONTO
(A popular race day sandwich)

Read the story, then turn the page.

Two men born in Indiana with very similar names have both left their mark on the world. Ballplayer Edd Roush, born in 1893, grew up to become a baseball player who worked on multiple teams, including the Cincinnati Reds, the New York Giants, the Chicago White Sox, and the Indianapolis Hoosiers (a Federal League team). After growing up on a farm, he played in the minor leagues until he was picked up by the Chicago White Sox. In 1919, he was part of the World Series Cincinnati Reds team who defeated the Chicago White Sox in the "Black Sox" Scandal. He was inducted into the National Baseball Hall of Fame in 1962.

John Edward Roush, known as Ed Roush, was a politician who served in the U.S. House of Representatives. Born in Oklahoma, he moved with his family to Indiana and attended high school and college there. He stayed as an adult, serving in the Indiana state legislature before running for federal office, where he served for several terms, not always consecutively, in the 1960s and 1970s. He was defeated in his last run by Dan Quayle. During his time in office, he pushed hard for the passage of an emergency number. A test call in Alabama took place in February 1968, and the first call on AT&T's Bell System took place in Huntington, Indiana, on March 1st of that year. Ed Roush dialed 9-1-1 to make a call to Police Officer Fredric Dutt.

Indiana Aptitude Part II

(Do not read this until you have read the previous page!)

1. Edd Roush was part of this team in 1919.

    A. Cincinnati Reds

    B. New York Giants

    C. Indianapolis Hoosiers

    D. Chicago White Sox

2. Edd Roush was inducted into the Baseball Hall of Fame in this year.

    A. 1952

    B. 1962

    C. 1968

    D. He was never inducted.

3. Ed Roush made the first AT&T 9-1-1 call from this city.

    A. Washington, DC

    B. Huntington, Indiana

    C. Huntington, Alabama

    D. Indianapolis

4. This politician won an election against incumbent Ed Roush.

    _____

State Fair Trivia

How much do you know about the Iowa State Fair?

1. The Iowa State Fair is held at the Iowa State Fairgrounds in this city.
   A. Des Moines
   B. Dubuque
   C. Davenport
   D. Iowa City

2. Which of the following is a contest held at the Iowa State Fair?
   A. Pie eating
   B. Cow chip throwing
   C. Hog calling
   D. All of the above

3. The Iowa State Fair generally takes place during this time period.
   A. Memorial Day weekend
   B. A span of about ten days that includes July 4
   C. A span of about eleven days in August
   D. A span of about five days including Labor Day weekend

4. This animal is traditionally sculpted out of butter at the state fair.
   A. Dog
   B. Cow
   C. Sheep
   D. Horse

Answers on page 148.

Searching Iowa

AMANA COLONIES

AMES

BURR OAK
(State tree)

CEDAR RAPIDS

CORN BELT

DAVENPORT

DES MOINES

EASTERN GOLDFINCH
(State bird)

GEODE
(State rock)

GRANT WOOD

IOWA CITY

MADISON COUNTY

MAMIE EISENHOWER

MISSISSIPPI
(River)

MISSOURI
(River)

PRAIRIE ROSE
(State flower)

SIOUX CITY

WRITERS' WORKSHOP

```
E I A H R Q B I O W A C I T Y G
X P J H A S E N I O M S E D G L
E A S T E R N G O L D F I N C H
R L D O O W T N A R G A B X P T
Q J S E I N O L O C A N A M A M
Y T N U O C N O S I D A M J C I
D N M M J M E H T M J B Z R T S
B U R R O A K D L L R S A C V S
E S O R E I R I A R P M W V C I
P O H S K R O W S R E T I R W S
D A V E N P O R T S R L T Z S S
J H T Y W I C N I G U A T T P I
V T L E B N R O C E X C P C V P
Y T I C X U O I S O W W F I V P
I R U O S S I M N D O Y U W D I
R E W O H N E S I E E I M A M S
```

Kansas Places

Match each site to its description.

1. **Fort Larned**

2. **Nicodemus**

3. **Dodge City**

4. **Topeka**

A. The oldest Black settlement west of the Mississippi River

B. Army post on the Santa Fe Trail

C. Home of the Brown vs. Board of Education National Historic Site

D. Near this former frontier town, you can still see the ruts of the Santa Fe Trail

Read the story, then turn the page.

The man who later was sometimes nicknamed the "Kansas Cyclone"— though better known as Ike—was actually born in Texas. Dwight Eisenhower's father David had Kansas roots, though, and his parents met (and later married) at Lane University in Kansas. During a time of financial difficulty, the family briefly moved to Texas, and it was during those years that Dwight Eisenhower was born in 1890, one of seven sons. In 1892, the family moved to Abilene, Kansas, where Ike grew up and attended high school. His mother Ida Stover Eisenhower was a reader with an interest in history, and Dwight became one as well.

While Eisenhower lived and worked in many different locations during his adulthood, he was buried in Abilene alongside his wife Mamie and one of their sons. The Dwight D. Eisenhower Presidential Library, Museum and Boyhood Home is also found there. The museum was begun even before Ike took office, to commemorate his role as Supreme Commander of Allied Forces in Europe. Construction of the library began in 1958, during Eisenhower's years in office.

Dog-loving visitors to Abilene may also be interested in seeing the Greyhound Hall of Fame that is also located there. Those flying into Kansas might use Wichita Dwight D. Eisenhower National airport, renamed after its favored son in 2014.

The Man from Kansas Part II

(Do not read this until you have read the previous page!)

1. Eisenhower's parents were named:
    A. Daniel and Ida
    B. David and Ida
    C. Dwight and Ida
    D. David and Mamie

2. Eisenhower was born in this year.
    A. 1870
    B. 1880
    C. 1890
    D. 1900

3. A Hall of Fame celebrating this dog breed is found in Eisenhower's hometown of Abilene.
    A. Mastiffs
    B. Dalmatians
    C. Police dogs
    D. Greyhounds

4. The airport was renamed in this year to include Eisenhower's name.
    A. 1952
    B. 1958
    C. 1978
    D. 2014

Unscramble each word or phrase below to reveal the name of a person who was born or later lived in Kentucky.

BEADLE ONION
(Explorer)

COOLERS YEOMANRY
(Singer, actress)

GREATLY CLAYS
(Singer)

A MIND JUDO
(Singer)

AHEAD MIL MUM
(Sports hero)

BANJO HUMANE JUDOS
(Naturalist)

RADAR LANDS HENS
(AKA The Colonel)

BARN WILLOW
(Aviator, the first Black woman to earn a pilot's license in the U.S.)

Answers on page 149.

AFFIRMED

AMERICAN PHAROAH

ANSEL WILLIAMSON
(First winning trainer)

ARISTIDES
(First winning horse)

BURGOO

CALUMET FARM

CHURCHILL DOWNS

GALLANT FOX

JUSTIFY

LOUISVILLE

MILLIONAIRE'S ROW

MINT JULEP

OLIVER LEWIS
(First winning jockey)

RIDERS UP

RUN FOR THE ROSES

SEATTLE SLEW

SECRETARIAT

THOROUGHBREDS

TRIPLE CROWN

WAR ADMIRAL

```
S  S  I  W  E  L  R  E  V  I  L  O  G  P  M  D  W  S
E  X  H  L  A  R  I  M  D  A  R  A  W  I  G  S  E  D
S  O  W  A  D  B  Z  F  F  B  N  K  L  S  A  N  L  E
O  F  N  K  O  B  U  R  G  O  O  L  M  R  V  S  S  R
R  T  D  W  N  R  E  C  U  P  I  T  I  E  N  W  E  B
E  N  E  S  O  Z  A  W  A  O  Y  S  M  W  A  X  L  H
H  A  M  P  T  R  H  H  N  L  T  F  O  S  R  R  T  G
T  L  R  F  M  L  C  A  P  I  U  D  I  I  B  B  T  U
R  L  I  Z  F  K  I  E  D  N  L  M  D  T  T  W  A  O
O  A  F  J  T  R  D  E  L  L  A  E  E  C  S  V  E  R
F  G  F  Q  E  V  S  Q  I  P  R  C  A  T  H  U  S  O
N  G  A  S  O  I  S  H  P  S  I  X  I  W  F  A  J  H
U  H  R  E  R  T  C  M  U  I  M  R  F  R  F  A  P  T
R  O  P  F  Y  R  C  P  T  Q  P  C  T  G  E  Y  R  U
W  U  T  T  U  E  L  L  I  V  S  I  U  O  L  M  P  M
R  D  P  H  S  E  C  R  E  T  A  R  I  A  T  K  A  K
K  Q  C  N  O  S  M  A  I  L  L  I  W  L  E  S  N  A
Y  Y  U  G  F  M  I  N  T  J  U  L  E  P  X  X  Q  X
```

Trip to the Big Easy

Across

1. Spring
5. Inflationary device
9. Simba's set
14. Actor _____ Ray in "Battle Cry"
15. Maturation agent
16. "Able was _____ saw Elba"
17. The center of Louisiana Cajun country in New Orleans
20. Baronial
21. Had a snack
22. This year's grads: abbr.
23. Creepy sounding canal
24. Acid-tongued
26. It began as a Native American trading post in New Orleans
32. Emeril Lagasse, for one
35. Zadora in "Fake-Out"
36. Gray-brown
37. Kareem, at UCLA
38. Swathe
41. Place for a recliner
42. Low form of life
44. Loire island
45. _____ the line (obeyed)
46. One of the "must-see" locations in the French Quarter of New Orleans
50. Either of two O.T. books
51. Calculating ones?
54. It's usually next to the F1 key
57. Fish stick?
58. "Gentlemen Prefer Blondes" heroine
61. It preserves the legacy of rituals, zombies, and gris-gris in New Orleans
64. Sound
65. Cutting part
66. Massachusetts motto word: Lat.
67. Cook veggies
68. Broadway beacon
69. Aptitude _____

Down

1. Test spots
2. Gentry
3. "To _____ friend of the good Duke of York's...": Shak.
4. Roman Catholic pope
5. Milkmaid's need
6. Loathsome
7. Blanc or Brooks
8. Evangelize
9. Erudite
10. Comparative ending
11. They lack refinement
12. _____-do-well
13. Makes a lap
18. Slue
19. Derive
24. Early resident of New Orleans
25. Lingerie item
27. Environmental agency: abbr.
28. Diarist Anais
29. Acclaim
30. Triangular blade
31. Lean in one direction
32. Welcome a keynoter
33. Bi-inverse
34. Pitcher of puzzles
38. Lavatory
39. Entirety
40. Hair-care product
43. DUI determinant: abbr.
45. Do a printer's task

47. Switch back?
48. Drenched
49. Off-white
52. Coeur d' _____, Idaho
53. "If I Ran the Zoo" author
54. Itinerary data
55. Put a lid on

56. Homophone of seed
58. Ford oval, e.g.
59. Sign to heed
60. "_____ a Man": Ciardi
62. Road to Rome
63. Auden's "To My Pupils," e.g.

Answers on page 149.

Musician Match

Match each Louisiana musician to their description.

1. Slim Harpo

2. Louis Armstrong

3. Charles Buddy Bolden

4. Fats Domino

A. Born in New Orleans in 1901, he was both a singer and a virtuoso trumpet player.

B. Born James Isaac Moore, this master of the "swamp blues" was known for his harmonica playing.

C. Born in 1877 in New Orleans, this cornet player helped shape ragtime into jazz.

D. This rock 'n' roll pioneer popularized the song "Blueberry Hill."

A Maine Symbol

Cryptograms are messages in substitution code. Break the code to read the message. For example, THE SMART CAT might become FVO QWGDF JGF if **F** is substituted for **T**, **V** for **H**, **O** for **E**, and so on.

"RGTJGKF" KO FGP GFDX PBZ FWEZ GU W NGDDZLZ

KF EWKFZ RQP PBZ PKPDZ UGM KPO GUUKNKWD

OPWPZ OBKH, W ONBGGFZM RQKDP KF ZWOP RGG-

PBRWX KF 1921 UGM PBZ HQMHGOZO GU WMNPKN

ZVHDGMWPKGF. OBZ EWJZ EGMZ PBWF 25 PMKHO

WRGSZ PBZ WMNPKN NKMNDZ, WFJ KO OPKDD KF

QOZ WO W PMWKFKFL OBKH.

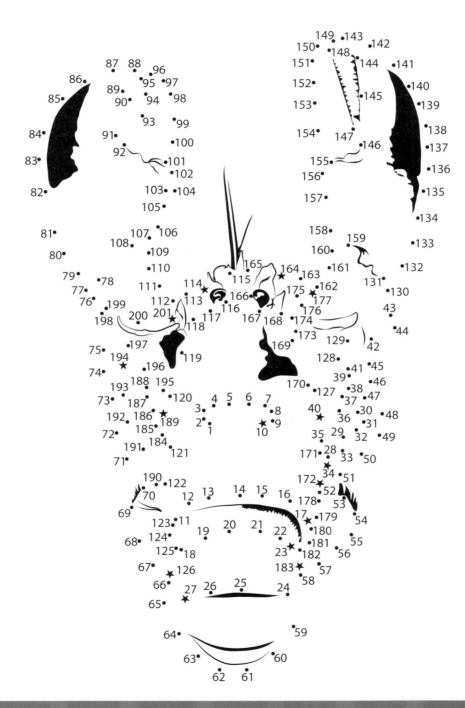

Ways to Get to Maryland

Change just one letter on each line to go from the top word to the bottom word. Do not change the order of the letters. You must have a common English word at each step.

MARY

—————

—————

—————

—————

LAND

Bonus:
Can you find another way to get to Maryland using a completely different set of words?

MARY

—————

—————

—————

—————

LAND

Answers on page 150.

More About Maryland

ACROSS

1. Works of beauty
4. Moms' moms, for short
8. "Savory beautiful swimmer" that the 10-Across is famous for
10. The _____ Bay, largest estuary in the US
12. Gaseous prefix
13. Economic improvements
15. Crusty pastries
17. Splash haphazardly
18. Actor Stephen of "The Crying Game"
20. Brainy sorts
22. Maryland is often called "America in _____"
27. "Can _____ least think it over?"
28. Digital reading, for short
29. Before, in a ballade
30. Big name in jazz
31. Do-say connection
32. The Sailing Capital of the World
34. BLT bread
36. Absquatulated
37. Sandwich shops, briefly
40. Industry bigwigs (var.)
44. Supporter of a strong, centralized government
46. Robber's run
47. Island known for its wild horse breed
48. The nickname given in 1919 to the state that opposed the prohibition law
49. Epps of "House"
50. Growler content

DOWN

1. "... more than one way to skin _____"
2. Ostrich-like bird
3. Pre-statehood area: abbr.
4. Mal de mer symptom
5. Snapchat or TikTok
6. Lacrosse targets
7. "Better Call _____" ("Breaking Bad" spin-off)
8. Use a thurible
9. Bean artists
11. Norwegian coin
14. Piercing, as a sound
16. Math offshoot
19. "... with _____-foot pole!"
21. Painter of melting clocks
22. Entree for a carnivore
23. Pointer Sisters "_____ Excited"
24. Water sprites
25. Banquet coffeepot
26. Hindmost
30. Eras upon eras
32. Topmost neck vertebra
33. Glib rapid speech
35. Bristles, to a biologist
38. "Make _____!" ("Star Trek command)"
39. Famous twins birthplace
41. Bit of marine life
42. "The Addams Family" co-star Julia
43. Captain Hook's henchman
45. Subway stop: abbr.

Answers on page 150.

Plymouth Ship

Solve this puzzle just as you would a sudoku. Use deductive logic to complete the grid so that each row, column, and 3 by 3 box contains the letters from the word MAYFLOWER.

	O		L					Y
	A			R	M	W	O	
			A					E
F			W					R
M		F		O				
		E		Y				
E			R					
A	W	R	M			E		
W				A			L	

Word Columns

Find the hidden quote from Massachusetts resident John F. Kennedy using the letters directly below each of the blank squares. Each letter is used only once. A black square indicates the end of a word.

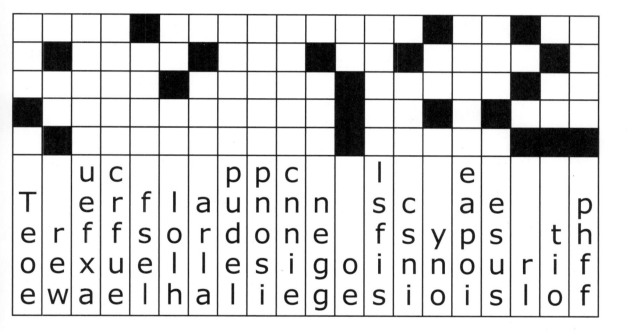

Answer on page 151.

ANN ARBOR

DEARBORN

DETROIT

DOMINO'S

DOW

FORD

GENERAL MOTORS

GRAND RAPIDS

GREAT LAKES

ISLE ROYALE
(National Park)

KELLOGG'S

LANSING

LIONS
(Football)

LITTLE CAESARS

LOWER PENINSULA

MACKINAC

MOTOWN

OJIBWE

PETOSKEY STONE

PISTONS
(Basketball)

RED WINGS
(Ice hockey)

TART CHERRIES

TIGERS
(Baseball)

UPPER PENINSULA

WHIRLPOOL

WOLVERINE
(College mascot)

YOOPER

```
K Z H C G R E A T L A K E S D O W H
T V G I R M B S D I P A R D N A R G
W I L W H I R L P O O L O J I B W E
T I O E L I T T L E C A E S A R S L
S I S R M R A O L D R O F U S S V P
K E G L T A L N R I N D P K R B U E
E U I E E C X N R M P V T O G X T I
L C C R R R D K O A E C J P T N Q O
L W J D R S O B I R R P P H O I K S
O W O Y N E R Y P N I B W D M S W K
G L R O O A H E A S A H O Q L N O E
G M I J E O N C T L Y C I R A A L Y
S L Z D L I P O T H E N Y O R L V S
A L U S N I N E P R E W O L E B E T
M K S S O S Y G R P A A H E N B R O
M L U Y S O N I M O D T W D E T I N
N L S G N I W D E R B J G T G T N E
A A T P M G Q J M O T O W N A V E U
```

65   Answers on page 151.

Travel Itinerary

The traveler is visiting five locations in Michigan. In alphabetical order, they are: Ann Arbor, Detroit, Grand Rapids, Lansing, and Sault Ste. Marie. Each location will be visited only once. Can you put together the travel timeline, using the information below?

1. The traveler visits the home of the University of Michigan immediately before going to the city in Michigan's Upper Peninsula.

2. The place nicknamed "Motown" is visited sometime after the state capital, but not immediately after.

3. Gerald Ford's childhood home, and the place where his presidential museum is located, is visited either first or second.

4. Grand Rapids is visited before Ann Arbor, but not immediately before.

5. Sault Ste. Marie is not visited last.

Read the story, then turn the page.

Every year, up to 14,000 visitors head to west-central Minnesota for Barnesville Potato Days in late August when this small town celebrates the lowly spud with a great menu of activities. The Potato Salad Cook-off attracts onlookers eager to compare the year's winning recipe with how Grandma used to make this popular picnic dish. Things can get messy during mashed potato wrestling, but the Miss Tator Tot pageant is much more refined. In 2021, contests for adults included potato peeling, potato picking, and a competition in sewing and stacking 100-pound burlap bags of potatoes. Contests for kids included a derby "potato car" race. Everyone could participate in a potato scavenger hunt and a mashed potato eating contest. Of course, there is plenty of food to sample, including Norwegian lefse, potato pancakes, potato sausage, potato soup, and traditional German potato dumplings.

Barnesville, tucked away in the fertile Red River Valley, has been honoring the crop of choice of many nearby farmers with this festival since 1938. The Red River Valley is a top potato-growing region.

(Do not read this until you have read the previous page!)

1. This town hosts the potato festival.

    A. Brownsville

    B. Spudsville

    C. Barnesville

    D. Barnestown

2. "Potato Days" started in this year.

    A. 1918

    B. 1938

    C. 1982

    D. 1993

3. "Potato Days" are held in this month.

    A. June

    B. July

    C. August

    D. September

4. This Norwegian dish can be eaten there.

    A. Lefse

    B. Lesfe

    C. Leffe

    D. Lesse

Minnesota Landmarks

Match each Minnesota landmark to its location.

1. Minnehaha Falls

2. Science Museum of Minnesota

3. Ellsworth Rock Gardens

4. Mall of America

A. Voyageurs National Park

B. St. Paul

C. Bloomington

D. Minneapolis

Answers on page 151.

State Symbol Scramble

Unscramble each capitalized word or phrase below to reveal one of Mississippi's state symbols.

LEAD REM
(Gemstone)

TATTOO WEEPS
(Food)

ENTREATS YORES
(Shell)

TEARING
(Rock)

American TAIGA ROLL
(Reptile)

GO ANIMAL
(Flower)

WE RENTS BE EYE HON
(Insect)

BALSA ERGS HUM TO
(Fish)

Mississippi Blues Trail

How much do you know about the Delta Blues?

1. The Mississippi Blues Trail has markers only in the Delta region of Mississippi.

    _____ True

    _____ False

2. The first marker placed honored this man called the "Father of the Delta Blues," Charley _____

    A. Waters

    B. Burnett

    C. Patton

    D. King

3. The second marker was placed at Southern Whispers restaurant on this street in Greenville, Mississippi.

    A. Nelson

    B. Beale

    C. Embarcadero

    D. Harlem

4. Legendary Delta bluesman Robert Johnson was born in this town, a site on the trial.

    A. Hazlehurst

    B. Clarksdale

    C. Dockery

    D. Greenwood

Answers on page 151.

Don't Miss Missouri

AMERICAN BULLFROG
(State amphibian)

ANHEUSER-BUSCH

BARBECUE

BRANSON

COLUMBIA

FIDDLE
(State instrument)

FRANKLIN
(Beginning of the Santa Fe Trail)

GATEWAY ARCH

HARRY TRUMAN

JEFFERSON CITY

KANSAS CITY

LAKE OF THE OZARKS

MARK TWAIN

MISSOURI FOX TROTTER
(State horse breed)

MISSOURI MULE
(State mammal)

OZARKS

PONY EXPRESS

RAGTIME

SANTA FE TRAIL

SHOW ME STATE

SPRINGFIELD

ST. LOUIS

```
L I A R T E F A T N A S I I I A A D
P H E V P K L E S K R A Z O M I C R
G A T E W A Y A R C H C H E B D E H
R E N I L K N A R F B I R M S L L A
S O G E A R Q L Y K B I U S S E U R
B H R M K V P A A C L J B E I M R
A A O H H J T N V A O X E A R F I Y
T E C W B S S B N C W Y L R P G R T
H Z M M M A I B R N F Q D B X N U R
J P H I S E U U I A Y P D E E I O U
R U F C T L S A O E N J I C Y R S M
Q W I X L G W T T L Z S F U N P S A
C T W F A T A A A V T C O E O S I N
Y C R T K C K R M T O S M N P T M J
D O P R A N H E U S E R B U S C H B
G L A K E O F T H E O Z A R K S C V
O M W X Y T I C N O S R E F F E J T
M I S S O U R I F O X T R O T T E R
```

Answers on page 152.

St. Louis History

Cryptograms are messages in substitution code. Break the code to read the message. For example, THE SMART CAT might become FVO QWGDF JGF if **F** is substituted for **T**, **V** for **H**, **O** for **E**, and so on.

PVL ULNI 1904 SNO N BQOU FEL WFI PVL YKPU. KP

VFOPLM BFPV PVL CFQKOKNEN GQIYVNOL LTGFOK-

PKFE, NCOF YNCCLM PVL OP. CFQKO SFICM'O WNKI,

NEM PVL OQDDLI FCUDGKY ZNDLO. DNEU FW PVL OK-

PLO QOLM WFI PVL ZNDLO, CKAL ZCLE LYVF YFQEPIU

YCQB, NIL OPKCC KE QOL PFMNU.

Montana Match

Match each event to the year it happened.

1. **Gold is discovered at Gold Creek.**

2. **Yellowstone National Park is created.**

3. **Montana becomes a state.**

4. **The transcontinental Northern Pacific Railroad is completed at Gold Creek.**

A. 1889

B. 1872

C. 1883

D. 1852

Answers on page 152.

Glacier National Park

Unscramble each word or phrase below to reveal a word or phrase related to Montana's Glacier National Park.

NO AUTOMATING
(Animal, symbol of park)

BYE RAZZ GIRL
(Animal)

REVILE OWN
(Animal)

ENTHUSING TOGO
(Road, engineering landmark)

PIG MANTRA
(Bird)

Western CARD DEER
(Tree)

FLING IF SHY
(Recreational activity)

QUA HER NIL
(Colorful duck)

Read the story, then turn the page.

Crafted in 1987, "Carhenge" stands as an exact proportional replica to the famed Stonehenge in England. Car for car to stone for stone, the measurements match up with precision, with a 1962 Cadillac matching Stonehenge's "heelstone." Close to 40 automobiles make up this tributary structure near Alliance, Nebraska. With some cars positioned upright, their trunks buried deep underground, and others settled into various contorted angles, this Stonehenge clone is complete with its coating of stone-gray paint.

Carhenge was developed by Jim Reinders, who later donated the site to "Friends of Carhenge." The site currently has a visitor shop and other pieces of car art in the "Car Art Reserve," and general admission is free—just be sure to go during daylight hours.

In 2017, Alliance, Nebraska, was part of the swath of the United States that was in the path of totality for a solar eclipse; this drew a number of visitors to Carhenge as a viewing site.

(Do not read this until you have read the previous page!)

1. What year was Carhenge created?
    A. 1962
    B. 1975
    C. 1987
    D. 2017

2. The piece was developed by this man.
    A. Jim Reinders
    B. Jim Reinholdt
    C. Jim Reinhart
    D. Tim Reindeer

3. How many cars are included?
    A. About twenty
    B. Almost forty
    C. More than fifty
    D. Three

4. What color are the cars?
    A. Their original colors, a variety
    B. Brown
    C. Gray
    D. White

Nebraska Knowledge

How much do you know about Nebraska?

1. Nebraska's capital and largest city is Lincoln.

    _____ True

    _____ False

2. Which statement is true?

    A. Nebraska has a bicameral legislature, with representives and senators.

    B. Nebraska has a unicameral legislature, with members called senators.

    C. Nebraska has a unicameral legislature, with members called representatives.

    D. Nebraska has a tricemeral legislature, with members called representatives, senators, and pioneers.

3. Scotts Bluff National Monument is important for this reason.

    A. It was the site of a famous gunfight.

    B. It was a landmark along several trails for westward pioneers.

    C. It was the birthplace of Nebraska's first governor.

    D. It was the state's first capital city.

4. This drink was created by Nebraskan Edwin Perkins and is the state's official soft drink.

    A. Pepsi

    B. Cream soda

    C. Kool-Aid

    D. Tab

Answers on page 152.

Knowing Nevada

ACROSS

2. An amazing equid seen in Nevada's Virginia Range
11. "Gotcha!"
13. Evil glance
14. Many-____ (polychromatic)
15. Computer attachment
17. "Please reply" letters
18. Exam part, sometimes
19. Forearm length, in biblical times
21. Avant-garde
23. The O of the OWN Network
26. Close to closed
29. You go to one when visiting 31-Across
30. Hearty greeting
31. The Las ____ Strip, most famous gambling street in the world
32. Hustle or bustle
33. Medieval catapult
35. Degree offerer: abbr.
36. Coastal wader
37. Broadway disaster
39. Garlic mayo
41. Nut to crack
44. Smokes, briefly
46. Fabricated
48. A neighboring state to Nevada
49. Shakespearean monarch
50. Word of support
51. Beautiful body of water in the desert famous for being the home of the endangered cui-ui fish

DOWN

1. Major tourist attraction and home to the mysterious underwater creature, Tessie
2. Mate of means
3. Frank Wright's middle name
4. Anti-crack org.
5. Forbearance
6. Language of Pakistan
7. Sap-sucking insects
8. Mozart's nationality
9. The Silver State: abbr.
10. Macroeconomics stat
12. "____ Just Not That Into You" (film)
16. Boxing champ Max
20. Burlesque wraps
22. Person on the move
24. Former Disney show "____ Mack"
25. Gigantic engineering project
27. Swiss psychiatrist Carl
28. Petri dish gel prepared from seaweed
29. Texas Hold 'em bet
31. White House "no"
34. Kimono wearer
35. "Once ____ a time..."
37. Penalized
38. La Scala offering
40. 1953 Leslie Caron role
42. Eyelid trouble (var.)
43. Shoebox ltrs.
44. Java holder
45. Absurd suffix
47. He played Batman

Answers on page 153.

Cryptograms are messages in substitution code. Break the code to read the message. For example, THE SMART CAT might become FVO QWGDF JGF if **F** is substituted for **T, V** for **H, O** for **E**, and so on.

AOJBZD UZQOL TOIO DZBOR Z DZNFEDZA BEDPBODN

FD 1922. NJO UZQOL ZDR NJO LPIIEPDRFDK ZIOZ TOIO

DZBOR Z DZNFEDZA GZIS FD 1986. NJO GZIS FL ZD

"FDNOIDZNFEDZA RZIS LSX GZIS" ZDR EMMOIL MZDN-

ZLNFU DFKJNNFBO QFOTL MEI ZLNIEDEBOIL.

Famous Residents

Unscramble each word or phrase below to reveal the name of a person who was born or later lived in New Hampshire.

ALPHA SANDER
(Astronaut)

JIG SLANDER
(Novelist)

POLITIC JUDO
(Novelist)

WRY TUBS KEBOB
(MLB pitcher)

MARE MONODY
(Actress, singer)

ALARM VARNISHES
(Comedian, actress)

RED MANDALAS
(Comedian, actor)

SWIRL ANTIHERO
(Early African-American novelist)

Answers on page 153.

New Hampshire Match

Match each place name to its description.

1. **Manchester**

2. **Concord**

3. **Loudon**

4. **Grover's Corners**

A. The site of the New Hampshire Motor Speedway

B. New Hampshire's most populous city

C. New Hampshire's capital city

D. This fictional New Hampshire town from Thornton Wilder's "Our Town" was reportedly based on Peterborough

New Jersey Folklore Part I

Read the story, then turn the page.

According to most reports, New Jersey's cryptozoological curiosity has wings, a horse's face, a pig's hooves, and a kangaroo's body. The legend of the Jersey Devil was born in the 1700s—based on a tale of a cursed baby-turned-demon that flew off into the night.

One of the first sightings of the Jersey Devil took place in the early 1800s when Commodore Stephen Decatur saw a bizarre creature flying overhead as he was test-firing cannons at the Hanover Iron Works. Decatur took aim and fired upon the creature overhead, striking one of its wings. The creature didn't seem to care that it had just been shot by a cannonball and casually flew away.

Tales boomed in the early 1900s, with supposed sightings all over the state. At the beginning of 1909, thousands of people encountered the beast in the span of a week. To this day, people report Devil sightings, mostly in the spooky Pine Barrens, an area of more than a million acres of forested land in central and southern New Jersey. So named because the area's sandy, acidic soil is bad for growing crops, it has proven a fertile home for an amazing collection of trees and plants. While some locals think the creature is truly a supernatural beast, others say it's probably a misidentified sandhill crane.

(Do not read this until you have read the previous page!)

1. The Jersey Devil reportedly has this.
   - A. A pig's face
   - B. A pig's body
   - C. A pig's hooves
   - D. A pig's tail

2. Naval hero Stephen Decatur reportedly saw the creature while doing this.
   - A. Sailing
   - B. During battle
   - C. Test-firing cannons
   - D. Hunting on vacation

3. This year saw thousands of sightings in a short time span.
   - A. 1700
   - B. 1812
   - C. 1909
   - D. 1932

4. The Pine Barrens are in this region of New Jersey.
   - A. Northern
   - B. Eastern and central
   - C. Western and northern
   - D. Central and southern

Princeton Trivia

How much do you know about New Jersey's Princeton University?

1. Princeton was founded as the College of New Jersey in this year.

    A. 1646

    B. 1746

    C. 1846

    D. 1946

2. Which two presidents earned degrees from Princeton University? (Pick two.)

    A. James Madison

    B. Grover Cleveland

    C. Woodrow Wilson

    D. John F. Kennedy

3. Nassau Hall, on the university's campus, was once the capitol building of the United States.

    _____ True

    _____ False

4. Which statement is true about The Battle of Princeton?

    A. It refers to a 1777 Revolutionary War battle.

    B. It refers to a battle during the War of 1812.

    C. It refers to an 1863 Civil War battle.

    D. It refers to a legendary rugby game.

Answers on page 153.

Carlsbad Caverns National Park

Every word listed is contained within the group of letters. Words can be found in a straight line horizontally, vertically, or diagonally. They may be read either forward or backward.

AGAVE

BATS

BIZARRE

CARLSBAD

CAVES

CHAMBERS

CHOLLA

DARK

FORMATIONS

GUADALUPE

GYPSUM

LIMESTONE

REEF

SHALLOW

SOTOLS

STALACTITES

```
S P Y G V H E C Y I H W W E E G
P K O L I M E S T O N E P E D A
D F A D Y W O K O N T U B U J J
J O G G V I N W Z O L U J S W X
F R A A S M L T D A R K T N T W
B M V E E E Y P D W W A F C O O
M A E B D J V A E U L S H R I L
U T T F F E U A L A P O S V D L
S I F S B G Y T C E L J R H A A
P O B Z A I M T R L Q G S R B H
Y N O E K M I R A N N E F E S S
G S K Z M T A K T J B Y J E L T
J Q K E E Z F F I A T N R F R R
F Z H S I M U V S L O T O S A N
O I R B A Y F U L K Q T L M C T
S R E B M A H C Q Z K L L L S B N
```

Travel Itinerary

The traveler is visiting five locations in Michigan. In alphabetical order, they are: Albuquerque, Carlsbad Caverns National Park, Gila Cliff Dwellings National Monument, Santa Fe, and White Sands National Park. Each location will be visited only once. Can you put together the travel timeline, using the information below?

1. The traveler goes from one of the two national parks immediately to the national monument.

2. The traveler visits one of the two cities first.

3. The national park that was designated a national monument in 1923 and a national park in 1930 is visited before the national park that was designated a national monument in 1933 and a national park in 2019.

4. New Mexico's capital city is visited sometime before either of the national parks, but not immediately before.

5. New Mexico's largest city is not visited last.

New York Sightseeing

Solve this puzzle just as you would a sudoku. Use deductive logic to complete the grid so that each row, column, and 3 by 3 box contains the letters from the words DAIRY BELT. When you have completed the puzzle, read the shaded squares from left to right and top to bottom to reveal a hidden message regarding something to do in New York City.

Hidden message: _____

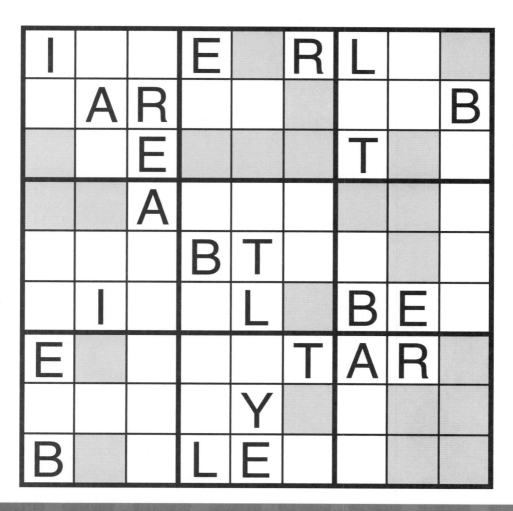

Answers on page 154.

On the Great White Way

ACROSS

1. Broadway musical with the song "Memory"
5. Broadway musical with "Tomorrow"
10. Hawke of "Dead Poets Society"
12. Crier of Greek myth
13. Broadway musical with "Hakuna Matata"
15. In ____ (somewhat)
16. Servitude
18. Beau for a doe
22. Enjoy a meal
23. Barrett once of Pink Floyd
25. Anger
26. NRA or NBA
28. Boring story
30. Sam Houston, to Houston
32. Broadway musical with "One"
37. "Fame" actress Cara
38. Kel's pal on Nickelodeon
39. Broadway musical with "Let Me Entertain You"
40. Broadway musical with "Seasons of Love"

DOWN

1. Prefix for whale
2. Greece airport code
3. Dance, music, painting, etc.
4. Spanish sauce
5. Raggedy ____ (some dolls)
6. Footwear with swooshes
7. "There's ____ in team!"
8. Former Saudi king ____ Saud
9. Brain scan (abbr.)
11. Physicist Bohr
14. 1955 hit by the Platters
16. Afternoon social event
17. Is down with
19. Source of bauxite
20. First word of "Scarborough Fair"
21. Berlin's country: abbr.
24. Copenhagen language, to natives
27. Bright crayon colors
29. William who directed "Funny Girl"
31. Bird of ____
32. Co. that was "too big to fail" in 2008
33. Shed a few tears
34. Cool, in the 1940s
35. A Bobbsey sister
36. Tolkien tree creature

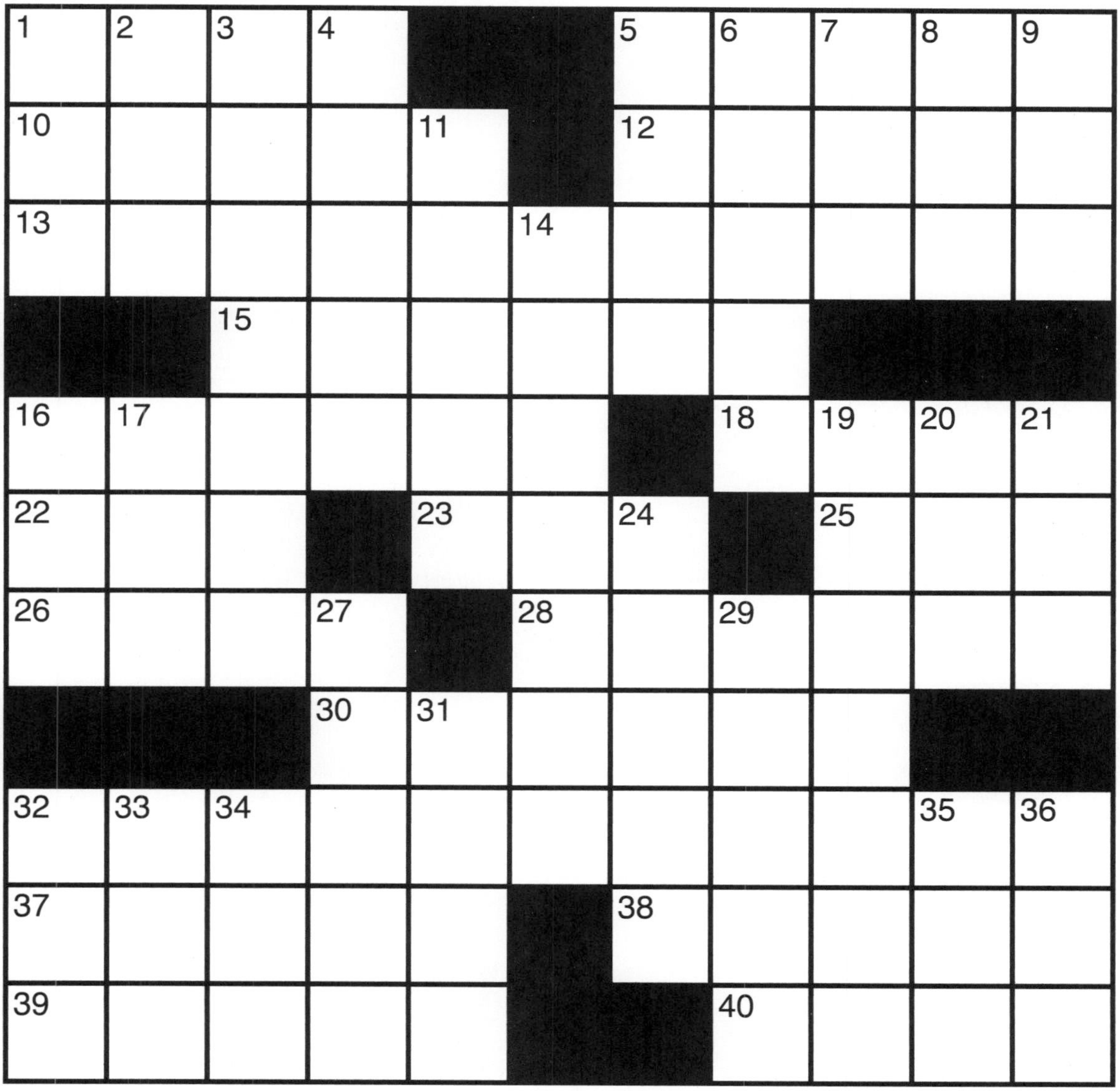

Answers on page 154.

ASHEVILLE

BARBECUE

CAPE HATTERAS

CHARLOTTE

CHEERWINE

DUKE UNIVERSITY

GOLDEN CORRAL

HARDAWAY SITE

HORNETS
(Basketball)

HURRICANES
(Ice hockey)

JAMES TAYLOR

JOHN COLTRANE

KRISPY KREME

MERLEFEST

NASCAR HALL OF FAME

NINA SIMONE

OUTER BANKS

PANTHERS
(Football)

RALEIGH

RESEARCH TRIANGLE PARK

SCUPPERNONG GRAPE
(State food)

SEAGROVE POTTERY

SHAG
(State dance)

TAR HEEL

```
G H A R D A W A Y S I T E J F H Y Y K R
D S Y H Y M X J F Y I T J L W F R R E P
G C T E P N I N A S I M O N E E T S C H
A U I M T A D R P M D N Y J T G E H O G
H P S E E N N S S G E S B T I A D R T R
S P R R A L F T A E W S O V R X N Z S I
J E E K Y R L E H R N P T C R E S W E N
O R V Y U N E I S E E A H A T Q X E F E
H N I P O R S V V V R T C S Y L W D E U
N O N S F I B A O E R S T I I L E Y L C
C N U I Q D C R L I H T W A R R O O R E
O G E R P I G E A D Y S V M H R E R E B
L G K K I A E N X I T X A R J E U H M R
T R U F E H G K I H G I E L A R P H T A
R A D S R L S K N A B R E T U O V A I B
A P G A E J Q R X T Y N M K W U N U C C
N E T P N A S C A R H A L L O F F A M E
E Z A I A Q T C N N H C H E E R W I N E
U R R G Q U T P L A R R O C N E D L O G
K B U A C E T T O L R A H C G F E Y Y C
```

Wright Flight

Cryptograms are messages in substitution code. Break the code to read the message. For example, THE SMART CAT might become FVO QWGDF JGF if **F** is substituted for **T**, **V** for **H**, **O** for **E**, and so on.

UMVHNP JMGPNLMO FQPVGFQD ELEGMVQD NGFGMO

PNL QEQZVFH LSLFPO PNQP PGGB IDQXL GF BVDD

TLSVD NVDD QP BVPPY NQUB VF 1903. PNL ELEGM-

VQD NQO Q OXRDIPRML, MLIDVXQO GC PNL XQEI

JRVDTVFHO, Q EGFRELFP, QFT EGML.

North Dakota Trivia

How much do you know about North Dakota?

1. North Dakota's capital city is:
    A. Fargo
    B. Bismarck
    C. Pierre
    D. Helena

2. North Dakota's state mammal is the:
    A. Grizzly bear
    B. Black bear
    C. Nokota horse
    D. Western meadowlark

3. North Dakota became a state under this president.
    A. Thomas Jefferson
    B. Abraham Lincoln
    C. Benjamin Harrison
    D. Theodore Roosevelt

4. North Dakota is home to this national park.
    A. Theodore Roosevelt National Park
    B. Badlands National Park
    C. Wind Cave National Park
    D. Black Canyon of the Gunnison National Park

Answers on page 155.

Great Plains State

Change just one letter on each line to go from the top word to the bottom word. Do not change the order of the letters. You must have a common English word at each step.

G R E A T

_____

_____

_____

_____

_____

_____ a small body of water

_____

_____

_____

_____

_____

_____

_____ to get up on two legs

_____

_____

_____

P L A I N

Presidential Anagrams

Seven of the nation's presidents were born in Ohio, and one more was elected from there. Unscramble their names below.

MENIALLY WHIR NOR HAIRS

STUNS ARGYLES

FURTHER ROSY HEAD

JEREMIAD FLAGS

JAMB NINE RASH IRON

MILKY WILL CINEMA

LLAMA IF TWIT

REDRAWN HARING

Answers on page 155.

Off to Ohio

AKRON

BENGALS
(Football)

BROWNS
(Football)

BUCKEYES

CAVALIERS
(Basketball)

CINCINNATI

CLEVELAND

COLUMBUS

CUYAHOGA RIVER

DAYTON

DORIS DAY

HANG ON SLOOPY
(State rock song)

JERRY SIEGEL
("Superman" co-creator)

JOE SHUSTER
("Superman" co-creator)

LAKE ERIE

OWENS CORNING

PAWPAW
(State fruit)

PLAYHOUSE SQUARE

REDS
(Baseball)

ROCK AND ROLL
(Hall of Fame)

STEVEN SPIELBERG

TOLEDO

```
I B U D N A L E V E L C L F U A D H
R D A V G B E N G A L S C J S H V K
P E Z L J O E S H U S T E R A A C K
L G D S Y B Q C D E Q N E K I N U L
A R Y S Z G U I E D U I R A L G Y L
Y E L E L N Q C D U L O K X Q O A O
H B E P L I J D K A N U J A P N H R
O L G D U N W I V E Y P A P A S O D
U E E I N R O A B W Y T B V Q L G N
S I I T H O C A R F A E O P K O A A
E P S A L C N Y O O Y P S N P O R K
S S Y N A S F A W B N K W C O P I C
Q N R N K N A D N J W O Q A F Y V O
U E R I E E R S S H R Z M A P O E R
A V E C E W Q I C O L U M B U S R S
R E J N R O C R O M K U U Y S E X T
E T B I I G C O L V X M M Q I C W N
V S W C E Q C D M D C T O L E D O M
```

Oklahoma's State Meal

BARBECUE PORK

BISCUITS

BLACK-EYED PEAS

CHICKEN FRIED STEAK

CORN

CORNBREAD

FRIED OKRA

GRITS

PECAN PIE

SAUSAGE
(and Gravy)

SQUASH

STRAWBERRIES

```
S S P B A P G R R V D G L M J L C
L Y T V E C S K P Q D E O M Y H P
B X C R R R C H E F T B B Y I K O
L C H F A A S G A B U T W C M A U
A S F L X W A U S I E O K U C Q F
C F T H K S B K M K Q E M O S B X
K B Q I U R L E Q S N C R L I Q W
E S Q A R C O Y R F Q N P J Y T P
Y H S J O G X R R R B N X D R N E
E W J R I Y F I E R I D Y W H U C
D V N D L J E U E U Q E C X S I A
P B S V O D N A I S C V S J A L N
E N D L S K D G A E O E X F U H P
A H N T W P D W P Z F Y B U Q Q I
S S E Q F C E B K N V G U R S M E
W A E A R B I S C U I T S J A T F
K V A R K O D E I R F M S S B B L
```

Cryptograms are messages in substitution code. Break the code to read the message. For example, THE SMART CAT might become FVO QWCDF JCF if **F** is substituted for **T**, **V** for **H**, **O** for **E**, and so on.

RZDN NE LII LECI WPUPOBV MBZLL? QULUN NPI EA-

BZPECZ WUNV COLIOC EK ZJN'L UDWJISUFBI WEBBI-

WNUED! EABZPECZ WUNV UL ZBLE PECI NE Z COLIOC

EK ELNIEBEMV, RPIJI VEO WZD LII PODSJISL EK LAIB-

INEDL EK ZDUCZBL—RUNP NPEOLZDSL CEJI DEN ED

SULGBZV.

Travel Itinerary

The traveler is visiting five locations in Oregon. In alphabetical order, they are: Beaverton, Crater Lake National Park, Malheur National Forest, Portland, and Salem. Each location will be visited only once. Can you put together the travel timeline, using the information below?

1. The traveler goes immediately from the location where Nike is headquartered to the site that hosts the International Rose Test Garden.

2. The traveler does not visit the state's capital or its largest city last.

3. The place that is home to a giant fungus that spans 3.4 square miles is not visited first or second.

4. Crater Lake National Park is not the fourth or last place visited.

5. One stop separates the visit to Salem from the later visit to the home of the Trail Blazers basketball team.

Answers on page 156.

Oregon Crossword

ACROSS

1. Org. with Colts and Chiefs
4. Business tycoons
11. "_____ degree"
12. Pretended to be
13. Highland boy
15. Often called the second most-climbed mountain in the world
17. Douglas-_____, Oregon's state tree
18. Quirkiness
19. Sight at Oregon winery
20. Mop the deck
21. Objections
23. Hanoi New Year
24. On, as a plane
26. Oregon nickname
31. Automatons
32. Parabolic path
34. Writes messily
37. Box for fun
38. Inland Asian sea
39. Red shade
41. Marsh product
42. Hunting targets during the annual Estacada Festival of the Fungus
44. Superlative finale
45. Low female voices
46. Removed
47. The crop that Willamette Valley is famous for
48. Pack animal

DOWN

1. Not exceeding
2. Predator-prey system
3. Having a tail
4. Damon of Hollywood
5. Feeling sore
6. Old Pontiac model
7. Abnormal new growth of tissue
8. Do the math, maybe
9. Pixielike
10. Peter or Patrick
14. Bride's purchase
16. Quill part
19. "Livin' La _____ Loca"
21. Sponge features
22. Crafts' companion
24. Openly declare
25. Summoner's cord
27. "I've Got _____ in Kalamazoo"
28. Pudding variety
29. Dutch Renaissance humanist
30. Inedible orange
33. Helmet toppers
35. Investor's worry
36. One with dreads
37. Sellout sign
39. French endearment meaning "cabbage"
40. Formerly, formerly
42. West of old Hollywood
43. Train depot: abbr.

Answers on page 156.

Blocks

The grid below contains 17 nine-letter words. Some of the letters are missing. Insert the 3-letter blocks into the grid to construct the words. If done correctly, the 2 gray rows will reveal a quote from famous Pennsylvanian Benjamin Franklin, reading top to bottom, left to right. Some letters from the 3-letter blocks have been provided.

A E R	E T E	R A N
A N E	F A N	R E S
A R Y	G N A	S E A
A T I	H T C	S E D
B E S	M M E	T E R
C E N	N C E	T O M
E N A	N C Y	T R A
E N T	P H E	T R Y
E S T	P R E	T U P

P	R	E						Y
			A			C	A	L
			N	O	M			A
A			O	P	L			
N	I	G				L	U	B
A	S	Y					R	
			N	S	I			T
	E		T	I	G	R	A	M
	E		E	N	T			
S	E	P				L	E	T
			R	N	A	L	L	Y
B	A	R	O	M	E			
			E	E	C	H	E	D
E	P	I				I	Z	E
			I	D	E			E
E						G	E	D
				E		S	O	N

Answers on page 156.

Pennsylvania Trivia

How much do you know about Pennsylvania?

1. This is Pennsylvania's capital city.
    A. Philadelphia
    B. Pittsburgh
    C. Harrisburg
    D. Hazleton

2. The scientific name of Pennsylvania's state insect is "Photuris pensylvanica." What is its common name?
    A. Lightning bug
    B. Western honeybee
    C. Stink beetle
    D. Ladybug

3. Which statement about the founder of the colony of Pennsylvania is true?
    A. William Penn was a Quaker.
    B. Wiliam Penn was Amish.
    C. William Penn was a Puritan.
    D. William Penn was a Catholic.

4. Which of the following historical sites is located in Pennsylvania?
    A. Valley Forge
    B. Gettysburg
    C. Fort Necessity
    D. All of the above

Read the story, then turn the page.

It's a piece of baseball history: the game that took eight hours, 25 minutes, and 33 innings to play, and it took place in Rhode Island. While many of the players who suited up for the Class AAA epic between the Pawtucket Red Sox and Rochester Red Wings on April 18, 1981, later saw action in the majors, including Wade Boggs and Cal Ripken, this is one minor-league contest they would never forget.

The "PawSox"—Boston's top farm club, led by star third baseman Wade Boggs—played host for the game, which began on a cold and windy Rhode Island night before 1,740 fans at McCoy Stadium. They watched the visitors (affiliates of the Baltimore Orioles) take a 1-0 lead in the seventh, but Pawtucket knotted the score in the ninth. There the seemingly endless string of zeroes on the scoreboard began, altered only with matching "1s" when both teams scored in the 21st.

Conditions grew so frigid after midnight that pitchers broke up benches and lit fires in the bullpen. Umpires could not find a rule about International League curfews, so action continued until league president Harold Cooper suspended play after 32 innings at 4:07 a.m. on Easter Sunday. Only 19 fans remained.

The 2-2 contest made national headlines. By the time play resumed on June 23, Major League Baseball players were on strike, so reporters descended 140 strong on Pawtucket. They were joined by a sellout crowd of 5,746, who waited just 18 minutes before Dave Koza singled in Marty Barrett to give Pawtucket a 3-2 victory in the bottom of the 33rd.

(Do not read this until you have read the previous page!)

1. The game took place in this Rhode Island stadium.

> A. McCoy
>
> B. McKay
>
> C. Pawtucket
>
> D. Rochester

2. The game lasted this many innings.

> A. 13
>
> B. 21
>
> C. 32
>
> D. 33

3. This team won.

> A. Pawtucket Red Sox
>
> B. Rochester Red Wings
>
> C. Pawtucket Red Wings
>
> D. Rochester Red Sox

4. This was the final score.

> A. 1-0
>
> B. 2-1
>
> C. 3-2
>
> D. 3-3

Rhode Island Match

Match each event to the year it happened.

1. **Banished from Massachusetts Bay Colony, Roger Williams makes arrangements with the chief of the Narragansett tribe to settle at Narragansett Bay**

2. **Revolutionaries burn the British ship "HMS Gaspee."**

3. **The First Rhode Island Regiment is formed.**

4. **Brown University is founded.**

A. 1772

B. 1764

C. 1636

D. 1775

Answers on page 157.

South Carolina Search

BLUE RIDGE MOUNTAINS

BOYKIN SPANIEL
(State dog breed)

CAESARS HEAD
(State park)

CHARLESTON

CLEMSON

COLUMBIA

DARLINGTON RACEWAY

EARTHA KITT

HILTON HEAD

LOWCOUNTRY

MYRTLE BEACH

PALMETTO STATE

PAT CONROY

SEA ISLANDS

SPOLETO FESTIVAL

STEPHEN COLBERT

THE CITADEL

VANNA WHITE

```
B T R E B L O C N E H P E T S S K J
S L U L Z N M C H P V C K N H N Y A
S Y U Z A R C F L A A A I C F A Q C
I E U E C V L A N E B Q A I W O Z S
C F A S R N I N E Y M E J E P Q U E
C H B I X I A T O S B S C L P W H A
O I A D S W D R S E A A O A U I D R
L R F R H L N G L E R R L N L F Z T
U O A I L O A T E N F M S T W U Y H
M Y T Q C E R N O M E O H K S E A
B E C T M Y S T D T O N T I E R G K
I Y A X M G G T T S H U N E T A Z I
A P G R Y N Q O O E M W N D L V D T
B O Y K I N S P A N I E L T M O W T
J Y H L M T R D N L N Z S G A T P T
H I R Q A S N U D X T L Z Z H I S S
B A R T L O W C O U N T R Y V E N V
D Q E S T H E C I T A D E L F O B S
```

Answers on page 157.

South Carolina Scramble

Unscramble each word or phrase below to reveal a word, phrase, or name related to South Carolina.

LUCIA MOB
(Capital)

ARMADA LENS
(State amphibian)

CLANGED SORREL
(State vegetable)

THY TEAMS
(State mineral/gem)

ROMANIA ELK
(Body of water)

GO CAREEN
(National Park)

MID SNOW BACKACHE
(Actor)

AMBER TROLLS
(Engineered a dramatic escape from slavery; served in the U.S. House of Representatives)

A South Dakota Law

Cryptograms are messages in substitution code. Break the code to read the message. For example, THE SMART CAT might become FVO QWGDF JGF if **F** is substituted for **T**, **V** for **H**, **O** for **E**, and so on.

FDDAOUJSI KA OJDG WQJKG JS "EAP DFS ILK FOOL-

WKLU VAO KGFK," JK'W JXXLIFX KA VFXX FWXLLR JS

F DGLLWL VFDKAOE JS WAPKG UFHAKF.

Mount Rushmore

Change just one letter on each line to go from the top word to the bottom word. Do not change the order of the letters. You must have a common English word at each step.

R U S H

_____

_____

_____

_____

M O R E

Read the story, then turn the page.

Created in 1925 by station manager George Dewey Hay, the Grand Ole Opry began as a weekly radio program that featured traditional "country" music, including folk songs and classic mountain tunes. In 1939, the show moved to NBC radio where it reached tens of thousands of listeners across the country. During the 1950s, the Opry was one of the nation's favorite radio programs, and with every song played on the Opry stage broadcast to America, Nashville solidified its spot as the country music capital of the world. Stars have included Hank Williams, who joined the cast in 1949; Pasty Cline, who achieved a lifelong dream when she became a member of the Opry; and Dolly Parton, who was booked at the Opry in 1959 at the tender age of 13 after appearing on a televised talent show.

One of the main characters was comedian Sarah Colley, known by her stage name Minnie Pearl. When she joined the Opry in 1940, 28-year-old Colley had no idea she would spend the next 50 years in show business performing as Minnie Pearl and wearing her trademark straw hat with the $1.98 price tag still attached. She later appeared on the show "Hee Haw."

(Do not read this until you have read the previous page!)

1. The Grand Ole Opry started in this year.

    A. 1919

    B. 1925

    C. 1939

    D. 1949

2. The program was created by this man.

    A. George Dewey Hay

    B. George Hay Dewey

    C. Hank Williams

    D. Hank Colley

3. Dolly Parton first appeared on the show in this year.

    A. 1939

    B. 1949

    C. 1959

    D. 1969

4. Minnie Pearl wore a hat with a price tag attached, showing this amount.

    A. 25 cents

    B. 99 cents

    C. $1.98

    D. $3.99

The Man from Tennessee

Solve this puzzle just as you would a sudoku. Use deductive logic to complete the grid so that each row, column, and 3 by 3 box contains the letters AEJKLMOPS. When you have completed the puzzle, unscramble the letters to reveal the 11th president of the United States.

L	E	M	M					J
	K				S			
O			L	P		M		E
		A				E		
P		S		M	K			O
		O		L		K		
		P		A	M		O	L
			E				M	
M			S					K

Deep in the Heart of...

A. J. FOYT

AUDIE MURPHY

BEN HOGAN

BUDDY HOLLY

CAROL BURNETT

CLYDE BARROW

CYD CHARISSE

DWIGHT DAVID EISENHOWER

GENE AUTRY

GEORGE JONES

HENRY CISNEROS

HOWARD HUGHES

JACK JOHNSON

JANIS JOPLIN

JOAN CRAWFORD

LARRY HAGMAN

LYNDON B. JOHNSON

MARY KAY ASH

MARY MARTIN

RED ADAIR

ROGER MILLER

SPANKY McFARLAND

TOMMY LEE JONES

TRINI LOPEZ

WILLIE NELSON

```
            H N O T S C Y D
            E L A L Y O N W
            R D N M Y O R I
            R E O F G S F M
            E R W N R A E J
            D C G O M S H R A I
            M E A B H R Y Y N C T S R           A E
            R N E R Y N R O R N F Y S A J F O P N E N C J
            O R I E O I E J O R S R H E G W I L L O E O E N
            G Y H S J L O S R T A P N Y J E H H S L A E O B
            Z R H S W H B H I N O L J D A R O L O N O S R R
            P E E Y S W Y U E E I M N A H H E R C O N S J S
            R N P A R I F A R F D A M R N N Y R G H J N A R
N S N A N S N N O A C Y O R L U U E N S I N Y E I A U O E O D E A Y
B T E A A R O I Y U A Y E L D H Y P S E H V I L W S J A S J L D N R
R K Y G S R S T K S D W I I R Y A D T T L A F E K J N J L O M K S
D C R O Y Y Y R A D E O T N F L D O L T O D C E H O I T Y N O D
N T D H R H D A M N U R H I S L I C R G A T O J M P H R R E N
R E A N A Y U M A A N R N R W O D O J H J H R O O L E H C S
R M E I E R K E Y M L T A A T L H E N B E E G W N N I M L O
C R I P B N G R R E R H B E D F Y N O G A A I S E C N T H
Y G H O E L     D A O A G E E E O D O R R L I W Y S S
Y E G W       B M U F B D D N R D D A C H D D C
            Y F Y C N Y S E H U Y Y C A E
            R R A Y M N L U I R B H
            L L A H Y G C N O A L
            S O J H K E C R E
            L R E B H N I H R
            S O Y T S A A J
            S E Y S G R P R
            N E O E S N S
            Y N N J A N
```

Answers on page 158.

Texas Trivia

How much do you know about Texas?

1. This Texas city is the most populous.
   A. Austin
   B. San Antonio
   C. Dallas
   D. Houston

2. The Texas official state flower is:
   A. The bluebonnet
   B. Texas sweet onion
   C. The flower of the Texas rainbow cactus
   D Blue Lacy

3. Oil was discovered at Spindletop in this year.
   A. 1834
   B. 1901
   C. 1912
   D. 1945

4. This city's motto is "The Live Music Capital of the World," and it hosts the South by Southwest festival.
   A. Austin
   B. San Antonio
   C. Dallas
   D. Houston

Utah Landmarks

Match each landmark to the place where it is found.

1. Delicate Arch, the arch seen on Utah's license plates

2. Two buttes called The Mittens

3. An incredible hoodoo called Thor's Hammer

4. A natural arch called Sipapu that spans 268 feet

A. Bryce Canyon National Park

B. Monument Valley

C. Arches National Park

D. Natural Bridges National Monument

Answers on page 158.

Zion National Park

ANASAZI

ARCHES

CONDORS

DEEP

DRAMATIC

GEOLOGIC

IVINS

KOLOB

LABYRINTH

NARROWS

PINYON

SHRUBS

SANDSTONE

UTAH

VIRGIN

ZION

```
X Q S E H C R A A A P E E D P B
U N C A E I L F X N S I K R C I
J B B E C G F W O A O I K U Z L
E I H M H I B E X S L Y H P K H
N K V K S C G N M A H V N A F N
O M B I L D X O N Z W S X I T J
T K X J N A B H L I R G P S P U
S H Y Z C S B A I O S K X U Z Y
D F X J L T J Y D H E H Q J S E
N C P Z X I J N R U G G D X W V
A L W O P V O U F I O P E H O I
S G M M B C B S U P N J C H R R
J B T W O S D R A M A T I C R G
Y U J Y L K X A W X Z H H V A I
H B R S O Z I O N B Z I Z E N N
V U Q R K P X A O X T B E G F L
```

Vermont Anagrams

Unscramble each word or phrase below to reveal a word, phrase, or name related to Vermont.

NEATEN HALL
(Revolutionary War patriot)

CAVILLED COOING
(Politician)

ALIEN RUN POX
(Novelist who lived in Vermont for decades)

ERMINE PLOT
(Capital)

CHAMP ALKALINE
(Body of water)

YUP SAMPLER
(Vermont is a huge producer of this food product.)

GOBLIN TURN
(City)

GERMINATE NOUNS
(Geographic feature)

A Milestone for the Nation

Cryptograms are messages in substitution code. Break the code to read the message. For example, THE SMART CAT might become FVO QWGDF JGF if **F** is substituted for **T**, **V** for **H**, **O** for **E**, and so on.

N SFBNE OKFB RZKBFEM, DXN BNV OPAAZK, SNL

MWZ ODKLM HZKLFE DE MWZ ENMDFE MF KZGZDRZ

N LFGDNA LZGPKDMV HNVBZEM. CFKE DE 1874, LWZ

SFKQZX NL N LGWFFAMZNGWZK NEX MWZE NL N

AZUNA LZGKZMNKV. WZK GANDB SNL MWZ ODKLM

MF CZ HKFGZLLZX DE 1940, N OZS VZNKL NOMZK LWZ

CZUNE HNVDEU DEMF MWZ LVLMZB.

Virginia Crossword

ACROSS

1. Flowering _____, the state tree
6. Relished
11. Sashimi fish
12. Hoist
13. Survivors, remnants
16. "A Doll's House" dramatist
17. One of the most photographed spots on the Appalachian Trail
18. To criticize harshly
19. Old photo shade
22. Certain believers
25. Relinquishing
26. Que. neighbor
27. Serpentine swimmer
28. End-of-page abbr.
29. Not as spicy
32. Poet's prayer
35. Did nothing
36. Laurel of comedy
37. "The _____ of a nation" (first settlements on the East Coast)
41. Sci-fi writer Asimov
44. Peter, frequent Poirot portrayer
45. H.C._____, Danish physicist who defined unit of magnetic field strength
46. Cleopatra's river
47. Neck areas
48. Escutcheons

DOWN

1. Campus quarters: abbr.
2. Black gold grp.
3. Festive event
4. Quick smells
5. Like twilight
6. Melodious
7. Labelled, like some folders
8. Grafton's "_____ for Evidence"
9. Bring into play
10. The largest office building in the world
14. Druid, e.g.
15. Movie preview
20. Spots on dominoes
21. "Come _____ play"
22. "The Old _____" (state's nickname, originally coined by Charles II in the middle of 17th century)
23. Oklahoma city
24. "_____ be a pleasure!"
25. Dusting items
30. Reduce in value
31. Royal decrees
33. Fully engaged
34. Like some skates
36. Earring types
38. Blue dye source
39. Lacking in affection
40. Nights before big events
42. Salty body
43. Dada co-founder Jean

Answers on page 159.

Famous Virginians

Unscramble each word or phrase below to reveal the name of a person who was born or later lived in Virginia.

HARSHER TAU
(Tennis player)

PLAYABLE IRE
(Actress and singer)

LANCES PITY
(Singer)

A LADYBUG GOBS
(Gymnast)

RECHARGE POP
(Computer programmer, U.S. Navy Rear Admiral)

A JASMINE MODS
(Politician)

AN NEWTON YEW
(Singer, entertainer)

ILK RILL MACAW
(Explorer)

Answers on page 159.

Seattle Trivia

How much do you know about Seattle?

1. Seattle is about this distance from the Canadian border.

    A. 5 miles

    B. 100 miles

    C. 300 miles

    D. 1,000 miles

2. Seattle was the birthplace of this musician.

    A. Jimi Hendrix

    B. Kurt Cobain

    C. Eddie Vedder

    D. Dave Grohl

3. The Space Needle was built for the World Fair held in this year.

    A. 1912

    B. 1942

    C. 1962

    D. 1982

4. The Seattle _____ play rugby.

    A. Seawolves

    B. Mariners

    C. Dragons

    D. Sounders

Answers on page 159.

Washington Words

EVERGREEN STATE

GRAND COULEE DAM

KENNEWICK MAN

KRAKEN
(Ice hockey)

LUMBER

MARINERS
(Baseball)

MOUNT RAINIER

OLYMPIA

ORCA
(Marine mammal)

OREGON TREATY

PACIFIC NORTHWEST

PUGET SOUND

SEAHAWKS
(Football)

SEATTLE

SPOKANE

STORM
(Women's basketball)

VINEYARDS

YAKIMA RIVER

O E P R E V I R A M I K A Y Z G K G
R J S E U R P L G C F G L P R R I M
P V I L D Y E U R A E F T A Q S Z O
B S O T I W V I Q B L W N S R P Q R
V K T T C N D C N S Z D D E T X M E
S K N A R U Z R K I C R N X I Y Y G
L R I E K C T W P O A I G O P T E O
M A W S M P A R U Y R R F C X N U N
S K E N O H U L E A X L T X A M F T
T E R R A K E N M H T X U N A C J R
O N C E M E I S R J U D Z M U I F E
R A S O D V I I O X Y D C L B O W A
M D A A I P M Y L O X G N L Y E M T
M F M L K E N N E W I C K M A N R Y
R K E T A T S N E E R G R E V E W P
G G Y J C Q S P O K A N E W H R Y C
I P U C I N Y G P U G E T S O U N D
C S T S E W H T R O N C I F I C A P

Answers on page 159.

Cryptograms are messages in substitution code. Break the code to read the message. For example, THE SMART CAT might become FVO QWGDF JGF if **F** is substituted for **T, V** for **H, O** for **E,** and so on.

SKLM QTJPTCTB RBL NEOJ ENNTFTBZ LMBMK LECPL.

MRK AELM JKFKCM, JKZKBLKI TC 1971 BCI ABIK B

LMBMK LECP TC 2014, TL VERC IKCQKJ'L "MBXK AK

REAK, FEOCMJW JEBIL."

Read the story, then turn the page.

Celebrations of mothers date back to antiquity, but Mother's Day proper was the brainchild of West Virginian Anna Jarvis. Raised in Grafton, West Virginia, Jarvis was the daughter of a woman who organized events called Mother's Friendship Days, which reunited West Virginia families that had been separated during the Civil War. After her mother died in 1905, Jarvis paid homage to her with an aggressive letter-writing campaign that began in 1907 and urged elected officials and newspaper editors to promote an official holiday to honor all mothers.

Within six years, most states observed Mother's Day. In 1914, President Woodrow Wilson signed a Congressional resolution that designated the second Sunday in May as Mother's Day across the nation. Jarvis herself came to deplore the commercialization of the holiday. She considered Mother's Day cards especially nefarious, opining that giving one was a lazy way to show appreciation for the person who gave you the gift of life. White carnations, incidentally, were the favorite flower of Anna Jarvis's mother, Ann Reeves Jarvis. Ironically, Anna Jarvis herself had no children.

Mother's Day Starts in WV Part II

(Do not read this until you have read the previous page!)

1. Anna Jarvis was born in this town.

> A. Wheeling
>
> B. Charleston
>
> C. Reeves
>
> D. Grafton

2. Woodrow Wilson signed a Congressional resolution in this year.

> A. 1905
>
> B. 1907
>
> C. 1914
>
> D. 1918

3. Anna Jarvis's mother loved this flower.

> A. Tulip
>
> B. Carnation
>
> C. Rose
>
> D. Chyrsanthemum

4. Mother's Day takes place on this date.

> A. First Sunday of May
>
> B. Second Sunday of May
>
> C. Third Sunday of May
>
> D. Last Sunday of May

The traveler is visiting five locations in Wisconsin. In alphabetical order, they are: Apostle Islands National Lakeshore, Green Bay, Madison, Milwaukee, and Spring Green. Each location will be visited only once. Can you put together the travel timeline, using the information below?

1. Wisconsin's capital city and its largest city are visited back to back, not necessarily in that order.

2. From the home of the Brewers, the traveler goes immediately north to the home of the Packers.

3. The place where the visitor can see both a Frank Lloyd Wright home named Taliesin and the House on the Rock is visited before the place that is home to Lambeau Field, but not immediately before.

4. The place with ice caves that is found on Lake Superior is visited after both the place on Lake Michigan and the place on Green Bay.

5. The place where you can see Taliesin is visited immediately before the place where you can visit both the Wright-designed Monona Terrace and the state's capitol building.

ADMIRALS
(Ice hockey)

ALDO LEOPOLD

BADGER
(State animal)

BEER

BREWERS
(Baseball)

BUCKS
(Basketball)

BUTTER

CHEESE

CHEQUAMEGON–NICOLET
(National Forest)

CIRCUS WORLD MUSEUM

CORN

CRANBERRIES

DAIRY STATE

DELLS

DRIFTLESS AREA

GREEN BAY

HOUSE ON THE ROCK

JOHNSONVILLE BRATS

LITTLE WHITE SCHOOLHOUSE

MARQUETTE

MILWAUKEE

MUSKELLUNGE
(State fish)

PACKERS
(Football)

POLKA
(State dance)

ROBERT LA FOLLETTE

```
L M F C S I Z T X N T S I K V R S O Y S
I U O I K L B S Q P Z U R Q I G Z R X R
T S D R C G A U H A G R E E N B A Y Q E
T K H C O X G R C X A K L O P S B C C K
L E D U R O E W I K U Y V L K K R H X C
E L U S E W S O A M S N T D H Z E E Z A
W L C W H F E N O V D A I K B Q W Y C P
H U B O T K E U Z H W A P F U S E B K A
I N S R N A H B B E D O S A K V R S B E
T G E L O D C R N C V A M F I A S N N R
E E I D E X D L O P O E L O D L A I I A
S D R M S I J V Z R G X K F O Q C T N S
C E R U U B L K E O E V X J E M O Z I S
H L E S O Z P T N M N L J G R C Y C B E
O L B E H Q T N A R R W S I N V Y A P L
O S N U Z U I R O N I G E C D I D N C T
L F A M B C Q C F Q J H V Z P G K X A F
H T R P O U B M I L W A U K E E K R O I
O F C L E F U R B E E R Q R F M H H G R
U L E T T E L L O F A L T R E B O R F D
S T T S T A R B E L L I V N O S N H O J
E E O O U K E D A I R Y S T A T E Z E N
```

Answers on page 160.

Wyoming Words

Unscramble each word or phrase below to reveal a word, phrase, or name related to Wyoming.

HENCE YEN
(Capital)

SQUEAL RIGHT
(State motto)

REGNANT DOT
(National Park)

IRONIC BASEMAN
(State mammal)

ERRATIC TOPS
(State dinosaur)

TWO SILVERED
(National monument, the first in the United States)

WAFT THEM OX
(Actor)

OH SHERBET STIR ARMOR
(First female judge in the U.S.)

Yellowstone Trivia

How much do you know about Yellowstone National Park?

1. Yellowstone is famous for its thermal features, including geysers, mudpots, and steam vents. How many are there?

    A. 92

    B. Between 250 and 300

    C. Between 500 and 650

    D. More than 10,000

2. Old Faithful is the tallest active geyser in the world.

    _____ True

    _____ False

3. Yellowstone is home to this kind of bear.

    A. Black

    B. Grizzly

    C. Both

    D. Neither

4. Yellowstone was signed into law as the first national park by this president.

    A. Abraham Lincoln

    B. Ulysses Grant

    C. Benjamin Harrison

    D. Theodore Roosevelt

Answers on page 160.

Answers

Awesome Alabama
(Page 4)

Roll Tide
(Page 6)

Answers may vary. ROLL, toll, till, tile, TIDE or ROLL, role, rode, ride, TIDE or ROLL, role, rile, tile, TIDE or ROLL, rill, rile, tile, TIDE are all possibilities.

About the Iditarod
(Page 7)

1. C. March; 2. A. Anchorage, Nome; 3. False. The first winner in 1973 took 20 days, 0 hours, but in recent years it is common for the winning competitor to finish in 8 or 9 days. 4. Golden Harness

Searching Alaska
(Page 8)

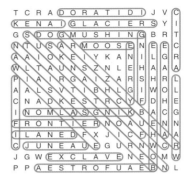

Grand Canyon
(Page 10)

Let this great wonder of nature remain as it now is. Do nothing to mar its grandeur, sublimity and loveliness. You cannot improve on it. But what you can do is to keep it for your children, your children's children, and all who come after you, as the one great sight which every American should see. —Theodore Roosevelt

Ancient Arizona History
(Page 12)

1. True; 2. C. 50,000 years; 3. B. Holsinger; 4. C. A National Natural Landmark

Arkansas Anagrams
(Page 13)

Ouachita; Bentonville; Bill Clinton; Billy Bob Thornton; Johnny Cash; Mockingbird; Hot Springs; Dillard's

Answers

All About Arkansas
(Page 14)

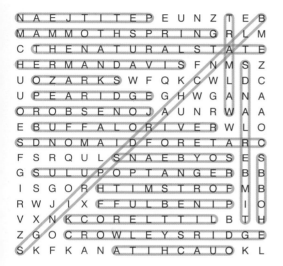

```
N A E J T I T E P E U N Z T E B
M A M M O T H S P R I N G R L M
C T H E N A T U R A L S T A T E
H E R M A N D A V I S F N M S Z
U O Z A R K S W F Q K C W L D C
U P E A R I D G E G H W G A A A
O R O B S E N O J A U N R W A A
E B U F F A L O R I V E R W L O
S D N O M A I D F O R E T A R C
F S R Q U L S N A E B Y O S E S
G S U L U P O P T A N G E R B B
I S G O R H T I M S T R O P M B
R W J I X F F U L B E N I P I O
V X N K C O R E L T T I L B T H
Z G O C R O W L E Y S R I D G E
S K F K A N A T I H C A U O K L
```

Famous Bay Sight
(Page 18)

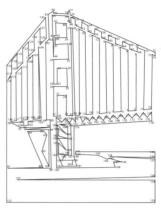

Mountain Peak Match
(Page 19)

1. D; 2. B; 3. A; 4. C

Steinbeck Classics
(Page 16)

¹V	²A	³L	⁴E		⁵A	⁶S	⁷P	⁸E	⁹N
¹⁰I	B	A	R		¹¹R	O	U	T	E
¹²C	A	N	N	¹³E	R	Y	R	O	W
¹⁴K	N	E	E	L		¹⁵A	L	I	T
		¹⁶S	B	A	¹⁷	¹⁸E	L	O	
¹⁹E	²⁰A	²¹S	T	O	F	²²E	D	E	N
²³A	L	E		²⁴W	O	R			
²⁵S	T	R	²⁶S		²⁷N	U	²⁸R	²⁹S	³⁰E
³¹T	H	E	R	³²E	D	P	O	N	Y
³³O	E	S	T	E		³⁴T	W	E	E
³⁵N	A	T	A	L		³⁶S	E	E	S

Denver Delight
(Page 20)

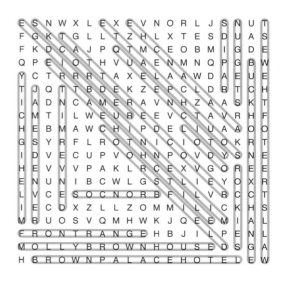

```
E S N W X L E X E V N O R L J S N U T
F G K T G L L T Z H L X T E S D U A S
F K D C A J P Q T M C E O B M I G D E
Q P E I O T H V U A E N M N Q P G B W
Y C T R R R T A X E L A A W D A E U E
T J Q T T B D E K Z P C L D R T C H F
I A D N C A M E R A V N H Z A A S K T
C M T I L W E U B E E V C T A V R H O
H E B M A W C H I P D E L I U A A O F
G S Y R F L R O T N I C I O T O K R T
E D V E C U P V O H N P O V D Y S N E
I M V I V P A K L R C E X V G E Y O X
L V C E S O C N O R B F I L V R C C H
E D C X Z L L Z O M M I L I C K H S L
M R U O S V Q M H W K J Q E E M I A L
F R O N T R A N G E H B J I L P E N A
M O L L Y B R O W N H O U S E D S G A
H B R O W N P A L A C E H O T E L E W
```

Answers

Connecticut Facts
(Page 22)

Connecticut Calling
(Page 24)

Some of Connecticut's nicknames are: the Constitution State, the Nutmeg State, the Provisions State, and the Land of Steady Habits.

Delaware Anagrams
(Page 25)

Dover; Wilmington; The First State; Joe Biden; Annie Jump Cannon; Blue hen; Rehoboth Beach; Bicycling

State Symbols
(Page 26)

1. A. Grey fox; 2. C. American holly; 3. C. Milk; 4. D. Peach blossom

Travel Itinerary
(Page 27)

The order is: Tallahassee (state capital), Jacksonville (Florida's largest city by population), Miami (southernmost city on the list, home of the Miami Dolphins and Miami Marlins), Tampa (home of the Tampa Bay Buccaneers, found on the Gulf Coast), Orlando (home of the Orlando Magic, closest to Disney World).

Our Largest Tropical Wilderness
(Page 28)

Answers

Going to Georgia
(Page 30)

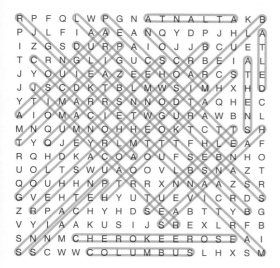

Off to Hawaii
(Page 34)

Peaches and Grits
(Page 32)

Answers may vary. PEACH, peace, place, plane, plans, plays, prays, trays, traps, trips, grips, GRITS

Island Hopping
(Page 33)

The order is: Hawai'i (where Mauna Kea and Mauna Loa are found), Kaua'i (home of Waimea Canyon), Oahu (the most populated island, home of Honolulu and Waikiki Beach), Moloka'i, Maui (home to Haleakala National Park).

An Idaho Animal
(Page 36)

Idaho's state fossil is the Hagerman horse, a very early equine that was first discovered in Hagerman, Idaho, by a cattle rancher. The first Hagerman horses lived about 3.5 million years ago.

Idaho History
(Page 38)

1. D. 1890; 2. False; Lewiston was the first capital of Idaho Territory; 3. B. Lewiston is on Pacific Time, and Boise on Mountain Time. 4. C. Coeur d'Alene

Answers

Chicago Skyline
(Page 39)

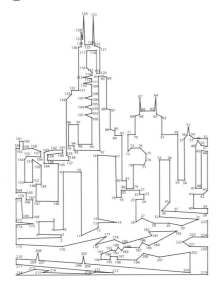

John Deere
(Page 40)

Indianapolis 500
(Page 42)

Speedway; Brickyard; Ray Harroun; Roger Penske; bottle of milk; Borg-Warner; Memorial Day; pork tenderloin

Indiana Aptitude
(Page 44)

1. A. Cincinnati Reds; 2. B. 1962; 3. B. Huntington, Indiana; 4. Dan Quayle

State Fair Trivia
(Page 45)

1. A. Des Moines; 2. D. All of the above; 3. C. A span of about eleven days in August; 4. B. Cow

Searching Iowa
(Page 46)

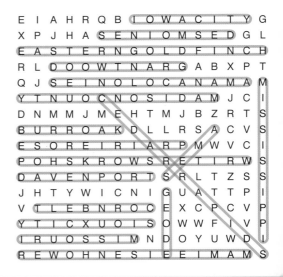

Answers

Kansas Places
(Page 48)

1. B.; 2. A; 3. D; 4. C

The Man from Kansas
(Page 50)

1. B. David and Ida; 2. C. 1890; 3. D. Greyhounds; 4. D. 2014

Kentucky Heroes
(Page 51)

Daniel Boone; Rosemary Clooney; Crystal Gayle; Naomi Judd; Muhammed Ali; John James Audubon; Harland Sanders; Willa Brown

Kentucky Derby
(Page 52)

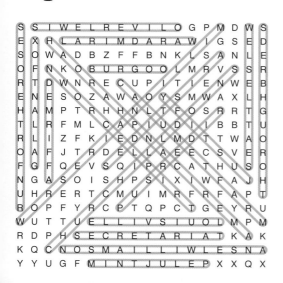

Trip to the Big Easy
(Page 54)

Musician Match
(Page 56)

1. B; 2. A; 3. C; 4. D

A Maine Symbol
(Page 57)

"Bowdoin" is not only the name of a college in Maine but the title for its official state ship, a schooner built in East Boothbay in 1921 for the purposes of Arctic exploration. She made more than 25 trips above the Arctic Circle, and is still in use as a training ship.

The Maine Event
(Page 58)

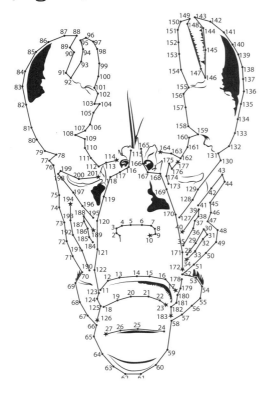

More About Maryland
(Page 60)

A	R	T		N	A	N	S		C	R	A	B
C	H	E	S	A	P	E	A	K	E			A
A	E	R		U	P	T	U	R	N	S		R
T	A	R	T	S		S	L	O	S	H		I
		R	E	A				N	E	R	D	S
M	I	N	I	A	T	U	R	E		I	A	T
E	M	A	G		E	R	E		E	L	L	A
A	S	I		A	N	N	A	P	O	L	I	S
T	O	A	S	T			R	A	N			
L		D	E	L	I	S		T	S	A	R	S
O		S	T	A	T	I	S	T		L	A	M
A			A	S	S	A	T	E	A	G	U	E
F	R	E	E		O	M	A	R		A	L	E

Ways to Get to Maryland
(Page 59)

Answers may vary. MARY, wary, ward, hard, hand, LAND or MARY, mark, bark, bank, band, LAND or MARY, many, mans, bans, band, LAND

Plymouth Ship
(Page 62)

F	O	W	L	M	E	A	R	Y
L	E	A	Y	F	R	M	W	O
Y	R	M	O	A	W	L	F	E
R	F	E	A	W	Y	O	M	L
M	A	Y	F	L	O	W	E	R
O	W	L	R	E	M	F	Y	A
E	M	O	W	R	L	Y	A	F
A	L	R	M	Y	F	E	O	W
W	Y	F	E	O	A	R	L	M

Answers

Word Columns
(Page 63)

"True happiness is the full use of your powers along lines of excellence in a life affording scope."

Magnificent Michigan
(Page 64)

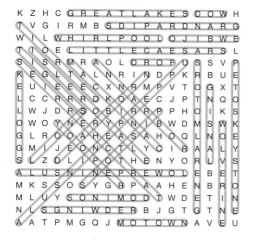

Travel Itinerary
(Page 66)

The order is: Grand Rapids (Gerald Ford's childhood home), Lansing (state capital), Ann Arbor (home of the University of Michigan), Sault Ste. Marie (Upper Peninsula), Detroit (Motown).

Minnesota Festival Fun
(Page 68)

1. C. Barnesville; 2. B. 1938; 3. C. August; 4. A. Lefse (Lefse look somewhat like pancakes; they can be rolled up lke a tortilla or wrap and contain sweet or savory fillings.)

Minnesota Landmarks
(Page 69)

1. D; 2. B; 3. A; 4. C

State Symbol Scramble
(Page 70)

emerald; sweet potato; eastern oyster; granite; alligator; magnolia; western honeybee; largemouth bass

Mississippi Blues Trail
(Page 71)

1. False. While many of the trail markers are found there, markers are found as far away as Chicago. 2. C. Patton; 3. A. Nelson; 4. A. Hazlehurst (He died in Greenwood).

Don't Miss Missouri
(Page 72)

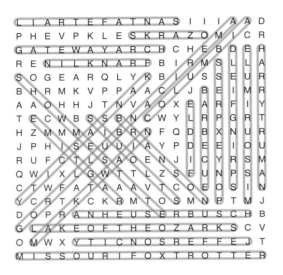

St. Louis History
(Page 74)

The year 1904 was a busy one for the city. It hosted both the Louisiana Purchase Exposition, also called the St. Louis World's Fair, and the Summer Olympic Games. Many of the sites used for the Games, like Glen Echo Country Club, are still in use today.

Montana Match
(Page 75)

1. D; 2. B; 3. A; 4. C

Glacier National Park
(Page 76)

Mountain goat; grizzly bear; wolverine; Going-to-the-Sun; ptarmigan; red cedar; fly fishing; harlequin

Auto Art in Nebraska
(Page 78)

1. C. 1987; 2. A. Jim Reinders; 3. B. Almost 40; 4. C. Gray

Nebraska Knowledge
(Page 79)

1. False. Its capital is Lincoln, but Omaha is its largest city. 2. B. Nebraska has a unicameral legislature, with members called senators. 3. B. It was a landmark along several trails for westward pioneers. 4. C. Kool-Aid

Answers

Knowing Nevada
(Page 80)

Great Basin, Nevada
(Page 82)

Lehman Caves were named a National Monument in 1922. The Caves and the surrounding area were named a National Park in 1986. The Park is an "International Dark Sky Park" and offers fantastic nighttime views for astronomers.

Famous Residents
(Page 83)

Alan Shepard; J.D. Salinger; Jodi Picoult; Bob Tewksbury; Mandy Moore; Sarah Silverman; Adam Sandler; Harriet Wilson

New Hampshire Match
(Page 84)

1. B; 2. C; 3. A; 4. D

New Jersey Folklore
(Page 86)

1. C. A pig's hooves; 2. C. Test-firing cannons; 3. C. 1909; 4. D. Central and southern

Princeton Trivia
(Page 87)

1. B. 1746; 2. A & C. James Madison and Woodrow Wilson both earned degrees, and Wilson later taught there and was its president. JFK did attend but he transferred to Harvard after several months; Grover Cleveland was a trustee. 3. True. Nassau Hall, built in 1754, hosted the Congress of the Confederation in 1783. 4. A. It refers to a 1777 Revolutionary War battle.

Answers

Carlsbad Caverns National Park
(Page 88)

```
S P Y G V H E C Y I H W W E E G
P K O L I M E S T O N E P E D A
D F A D Y W O K O N T U B U J J
J O G G V I N W Z O L U J S W X
F R A A S M L T D A R K T N T W
B M V E E E Y P D W W A F C O O
M A E B D J V A E U L S H R I L
U T F F E U A L A P O S V D I L
S I F S B G Y T C E L J R H A A
P O B Z A I M T R L Q G S R B H
Y N O E K M I R A N N E F E S S
G S K Z M T A K T J B Y J E L T
J Q K E E Z F F I A T N R F R N
F Z H S I M U V S L O T O S A N
O I R B A Y F U L K Q T L M C T
S R E B M A H C Q Z K L L S B N
```

Travel Itinerary
(Page 90)

The order is: Santa Fe (capital), Albuquerque (largest city), Carlsbad Caverns National Park, White Sands National Park, Gila Cliff Dwellings National Monument

New York Sightseeing
(Page 91)

```
I T B E D R L Y A
Y A R T I L E D B
L D E Y A B T I R
T B A I R E Y L D
D E L B T Y R A I
R I Y A L D B E T
E Y I D B T A R L
A L T R Y I D B E
B R D L E A I T Y
```

HIDDEN MESSAGE:
DALLY A BIT BY LADY LIBERTY

On the Great White Way
(Page 92)

C	A	T	S		A	N	N	I	E
E	T	H	A	N		N	I	O	B	E
T	H	E	L	I	O	N	K	I	N	G
			A	S	E	N	S	E		
T	H	R	A	L	L		S	T	A	G
E	A	T		S	Y	D		I	R	E
A	S	S	N		Y	A	W	N	E	R
			E	P	O	N	Y	M		
A	C	H	O	R	U	S	L	I	N	E
I	R	E	N	E		K	E	N	A	N
G	Y	P	S	Y		R	E	N	T

North Carolina Words
(Page 94)

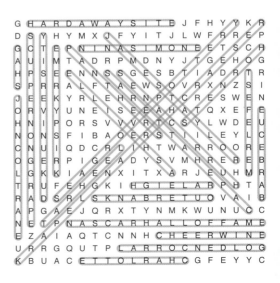

```
G H A R D A W A Y S I T B J F H Y Y K R
D S Y H Y M X J F Y I T J L W F R R E P
G C T E P N I N A S I M O N E E T S C H
A U I M T A D R P M D N Y J T G E H O G
H P S E E N N S S G E S B T I A D R T R
J E E K Y R L E H R N P T C R E S W E I
O R V Y U N E I S E E A H A T Q X E F N
H N I P O R S V V R T C S Y L W D E U C
N O N S F I B A O E R S T I L L E Y L E
C N U I Q D C R L I H T W A R R O O R E
I G K A E N X I T X A R J E U H W B T R
T R U F E H G K I H G I E L A R P H T A
R A D S R L S K N A B R E T U O V A I B
A P G A E J Q R X T Y N M K W U N U C C
N E T P N A S C A R H A L L O F F A M E
E Z A I A Q T C N N H C H E E R W I N E
U R R G Q U T P L A R R O C N E D L O G
K B U A C E T T O L R A H C G F E Y Y C
```

Answers

Wright Flight
(Page 96)

Wright Brothers National Memorial honors the amazing events that took place on Kill Devil Hill at Kitty Hawk in 1903. The Memorial has a sculpture, replicas of the camp buildings, a monument, and more.

North Dakota Trivia
(Page 97)

1. B. Bismarck; 2. Nokota horse; 3. Benjamin Harrison in 1889; 4. A. Theodore Roosevelt National Park

Great Plains State
(Page 98)

Answers may vary. GREAT, treat, tread, bread, breed, creed, creek, cheek, check, chuck, shuck, stuck, stack, stank, stand, staid, stain, slain, PLAIN

Presidential Anagrams
(Page 99)

Wiliam Henry Harrison (lived in Ohio when he was elected); Ulysses Grant; Rutherford Hayes; James Garfield; Benjamin Harrison; William McKinley; Wiliam Taft; Warren Harding.

Off to Ohio
(Page 100)

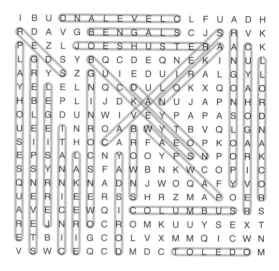

Oklahoma's State Meal
(Page 102)

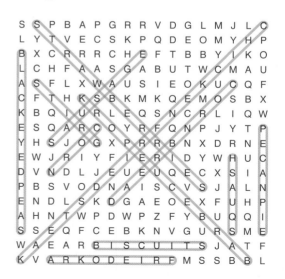

Answers

Oklahoma City Sights
(Page 104)

Want to see some Chihuly glass? Visit the Oklahoma City Museum of Art's incredible collection! Oklahoma City is also home to a Museum of Osteology, where you can see hundreds of skeletons of animals—with thousands more not on display.

Travel Itinerary
(Page 105)

The order is: Crater Lake National Park, Salem (Oregon's capital), Beaverton (Nike headquarters), Portland (largest city, home to the Trail Blazers and the International Rose Test Garden), Malheur National Forest (home to a giant fungus believed to be the largest living organism in the world).

Oregon Crossword
(Page 106)

Blocks
(Page 108)

Answers

Pennsylvania Trivia
(Page 110)

1. C. Harrisburg; 2. Lightning bug (also known as a firefly or glowworm); 3. A. William Penn was a Quaker. 4. D. All of the above

Rhode Island Baseball History
(Page 112)

1. A. McCoy; 2. D. 33; 3. A. Pawtucket Red Sox; 4. C. 3-2

Rhode Island Match
(Page 113)

1. C; 2. A; 3. D; 4; B

South Carolina Search
(Page 114)

South Carolina Scramble
(Page 116)

Columbia; salamander; collard greens; amethyst; Lake Marion; Congaree; Chadwick Boseman; Robert Smalls

A South Dakota Law
(Page 117)

According to Rich Smith in "You Can Get Arrested for That," it's illegal to fall asleep in a cheese factory in South Dakota.

Mount Rushmore
(Page 118)

Answers may vary. RUSH, bush (or rash), bash, base, bare, bore (or mare), MORE

A Nashville Institution
(Page 120)

1. B. 1925; 2. A. George Dewey Hay; 3. C. 1959; 4. C. $1.98

Answers

The Man from Tennessee
(Page 121)

L	P	E	M	K	O	A	S	J
A	K	M	J	E	S	O	L	P
O	S	J	L	P	A	M	K	E
K	L	A	O	S	J	E	P	M
P	E	S	A	M	K	L	J	O
J	M	O	P	L	E	K	A	S
E	J	P	K	A	M	S	O	L
S	O	K	E	J	L	P	M	A
M	A	L	S	O	P	J	E	K

Texas Trivia
(Page 124)

1. D. Houston; 2. A. Bluebonnet (the Blue Lacy is a dog breed that is the official state dog of Texas, and the Texas sweet onion is the offical state vegetable). 3. B. 1901; 4. A. Austin

Utah Landmarks
(Page 124)

1. C; 2. B; 3. A; 4. D

Deep in the Heart of...
(Page 122)

Zion National Park
(Page 126)

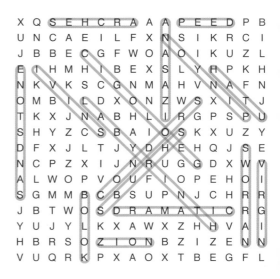

Answers

Vermont Anagrams
(Page 128)

Ethan Allen; Calvin Coolidge; Annie Proulx; Montpelier; Lake Champlain; maple syrup; Burlington; Green Mountains

A Milestone for the Nation
(Page 129)

A woman from Vermont, Ida May Fuller, was the first person in the nation to receive a Social Security Payment. Born in 1874, she worked as a schoolteacher and then as a legal secretary. Her claim was the first to be processed in 1940, a few years after she began paying into the system.

Virginia Crossword
(Page 130)

D	O	G	W	O	O	D		A	T	E	U	P
O	P	A	H			U	P	R	A	I	S	E
R	E	L	I	C	T	S		I	B	S	E	N
M	C	A	F	E	E	K	N	O	B			T
		F	L	A	Y		S	E	P	I	A	
D	E	I	S	T	S		C	E	D	I	N	G
O	N	T			E	E	L		P	T	O	
M	I	L	D	E	R		O	R	I	S	O	N
I	D	L	E	D		S	T	A	N			
N		B	I	R	T	H	P	L	A	C	E	
I	S	A	A	C		U	S	T	I	N	O	V
O	E	R	S	T	E	D		N	I	L	E	
N	A	P	E	S		S	H	I	E	L	D	S

Famous Virginians
(Page 132)

Arthur Ashe; Pearl Bailey; Patsy Cline; Gabby Douglas; Grace Hopper; James Madison; Wayne Newton; William Clark

Seattle Trivia
(Page 133)

1. B. 100 miles; 2. A. Jimi Hendrix. While the other three men have ties to Seattle through musical groups there, only Hendrix was born in the city. Cobain was born in Aberdeen, WA, while Vedder was born in Illinois and Grohl in Ohio. 3. C. 1962; 4. A. Seawolves. The Seattle Mariners play baseball; the Seattle Dragons play football in the XFL, and the Seattle Sounders play soccer.

Washington Words
(Page 134)

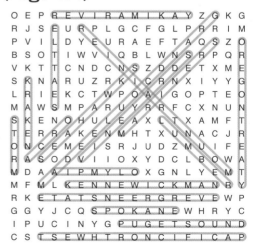

Answers

West Virginia Music
(Page 136)

West Virginia has four official state songs. The most recent, released in 1971 and made a state song in 2014, is John Denver's "Take Me Home, Country Roads."

Mother's Day Starts in WV
(Page 138)

1. D. Grafton; 2. C. 1914; 3. B. Carnation; 4. B. Second Sunday of May

Madison, Milwaukee, and More
(Page 139)

The order is: Spring Green (home to Taliesin and the House on the Rock), Madison (state capital and home to Monona Terrace), Milwaukee (largest city and home to the Brewers), Green Bay (home to the Packers, who play at Lambeau Field), and Apostle Island National Lakeshore (Lake Superior, ice caves).

Wonderful Wisconsin
(Page 140)

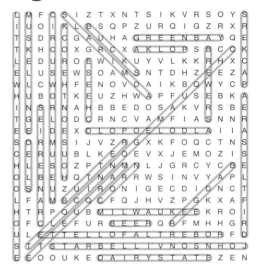

Wyoming Words
(Page 142)

Cheyenne; Equal Rights; Grand Teton; American Bison; Triceratops; Devils Tower; Matthew Fox; Esther Hobart Morris

Yellowstone Trivia
(Page 143)

1. D. More than 10,000; 2. False. That honor belongs to Steamboat Geyster, also found at Yellowstone; 3. C. Both; 4. B. Ulysses Grant